SIMON J. TAYLOR   Cathedral and
Continuing Ministerial Development Officer for the Diocese of Derby.
Prior to that, he was a parish priest in Bristol. He has a doctorate in
theology from the University of Oxford and has taught about the
Bible in universities, churches, a prison, pubs, cafés and tents.

HOW TO READ THE BIBLE
(without switching off your brain)

Simon J. Taylor

First published in Great Britain in 2015

Society for Promoting Christian Knowledge
36 Causton Street
London SW1P 4ST
www.spck.org.uk

Copyright © Simon J. Taylor 2015

All rights reserved. No part of this book may be reproduced or transmitted in any
form or by any means, electronic or mechanical, including photocopying,
recording, or by any information storage and retrieval system,
without permission in writing from the publisher.

SPCK does not necessarily endorse the individual views contained in its publications.

The author and publisher have made every effort to ensure that the external website
and email addresses included in this book are correct and up to date at the time
of going to press. The author and publisher are not responsible for
the content, quality or continuing accessibility of the sites.

Unless otherwise noted, Scripture quotations are taken from the New Revised Standard
Version of the Bible, Anglicized Edition, copyright © 1989, 1995 by the Division
of Christian Education of the National Council of the Churches of
Christ in the USA. Used by permission. All rights reserved.

British Library Cataloguing-in-Publication Data
A catalogue record for this book is available from the British Library

ISBN 978–0–281–07380–1
eBook ISBN 978–0–281–07381–8

Typeset by Graphicraft Limited, Hong Kong
First printed in Great Britain by Ashford Colour Press
Subsequently digitally printed in Great Britain

eBook by Graphicraft Limited, Hong Kong

Produced on paper from sustainable forests

For Jacky, Samuel and Ruth
with all my love

Contents

Acknowledgements

This book has its origins in material delivered at St Mary Redcliffe in Bristol and at Derby Cathedral. My thanks to all who listened and who offered me feedback.

At Derby Cathedral, I am grateful to colleagues who helped facilitate the course of talks in which this material came together for the first time, especially John Davies, Andy Trenier, Jackie Croft, Mat Mawson, Lucille Parsisson and Mandy Thomas. In the Diocese of Derby, my thanks go to colleagues in the Mission and Ministry Team, and to Lucy Harrison and Jo Armstrong, who created fabulous publicity for the talks. I am grateful to the Bishop of Derby, Dr Alastair Redfern, for his continued support and interest in the progress of the book.

Janice Price offered encouragement, belief and practical help in enabling this book to come into being. Paula Gooder was immensely generous in her faith in the project, in her advice and in writing the foreword.

At SPCK, Alison Barr was immensely patient and helpful to a first-time author. Neil Whyte's care and attention to detail at the copy-editing stage was astonishing.

Writing a book on the Bible has made me very mindful of those who taught me about it: my parents, Frances, Richard and Pam Taylor; my teachers, Simon Barker, Graham Haslam, Tom Wright and Sue Gillingham. The errors I have made are all my own responsibility and largely owing to not attending well enough to their instruction.

The dedication of this book reflects my deepest debts. Jacky has supported, cajoled and encouraged me at just the right times. She has read more drafts than can have been good for her. Samuel and Ruth continue to teach me in all kinds of ways. Their enthusiasm for my writing was best seen in their 'happy dance', performed when I first heard that the book was to be published. For all this and for putting up with me, thank you with all my heart.

Foreword

'Read the Bible,' we tell people; it sounds so simple, doesn't it? Just as we might read a nice novel, a letter from the bank or a message from a friend, the suggestion that we might read the Bible has an easy ring to it. All you have to do is pick it up and off you go. Anyone who has tried this will tell you that it is far from this easy. While there are parts of the Bible that fall into the category of 'easy reading', the vast majority does not. Some of the Bible is uplifting, but other parts are dull, bemusing, apparently irrelevant and sometimes even morally questionable (especially when it appears to condone genocide). So how do we go about reading the Bible?

One answer to this question is that what we need is a really good guide. Only the very foolish would attempt to scale a mountain without a map or to cook a dish never before attempted without a recipe. Even better than using a map or a recipe is being accompanied by someone who has scaled the mountain or who has cooked the dish before, and who offers tips along the way. In many ways this book functions as your own personal guide for the journey. It sets out what you need to take with you. It identifies which paths are easier to take than others and which routes might be better left until you have more experience.

As with all good guides, this book begins with what you need to know before you even start; it asks what you need to think about before you set out and looks at how to go about reading the Bible, and what hints and tips you might need to get started. From there, it moves on to what the Bible is, what story it is telling and how Jesus' own stories fit into this. Halfway through (at Chapter 5), it pauses to reflect a little more on how to pray with the Bible, since prayer is one of the main reasons you might be reading it in the first place.

The second half of the book turns to much more knotty problems; it looks at some of those really hard questions that many people ask but few people want to think about. Questions such as what does the

Bible really have to say about creation? And what does it say about money, sex and violence? How do we think about these very difficult and all too modern problems in the light of what the Bible says? We may not agree with everything we find here, but then this book is about reading the Bible without switching our brains off. The point is not about whether we agree with it all but whether we can work out what we think in the light of what the Bible says.

This is a book that will offer a guide to a complex subject, but it will also challenge you. It introduces you to the Bible as something that is living and life-giving. It calls you to set out from where you are and trust that the journey will be worthwhile. It summons you to an adventure, to a wrestling match and to a feast. If you would like to set out on the grand adventure of reading the Bible without switching off your brain, then this is a great guide to help you on your way. Proceed with caution, though: if you are going to read the Bible for all it is worth (as this book suggests that you do), only one thing is guaranteed – you will never be the same again.

Paula Gooder
Theologian in Residence for the Bible Society

Introduction

We present you with this Book, the most valuable thing
that this world affords.
Here is Wisdom; this is the royal Law; these are the
lively Oracles of God.

The Coronation Service[1]

With these words a Bible was presented to Queen Elizabeth II at her
coronation. I remember the first Bible I was ever given. It was an
eighth birthday present from my parents but I didn't really start to
read it until several years later. That Bible still sits on my bookshelf,
now betraying a good deal of evidence that it has been well read. The
cover sports a couple of stickers; some sticky tape holds the spine
together; inside there are lots of places where I've underlined or
highlighted passages. I don't use that first Bible any more. In time it
was replaced by a version more compatible with studying A-level and
university courses. This too is battered and held together with tape,
though I like to think the scribbles in the margins are a little more
learned these days!

Reading the Bible is an adventure. The great theologian Karl Barth
speaks of 'the strange new world within the Bible', which captures
my experience of Bible reading well. Reading the Bible has puzzled
me, challenged me, changed me, enlivened me. It has been a source
of comfort, frustration and of great insight. In this short book I invite
you to join the adventure and to find what the Bible can do for you
as you enter its strange new world.

The Bible is found in all kinds of places. There are novels based on
stories from the Bible – among my favourites are Jim Crace's *Quaran-
tine*, David Maine's *The Flood* and Anita Diamant's *The Red Tent*.
Hollywood has enjoyed making epic blockbusters out of Bible stories.
The 1956 Cecil B. DeMille film *The Ten Commandments*, the many
films of Jesus' life – of which my favourite is definitely Monty Python's
Life of Brian – and more recently Darren Aronofsky's eco-thriller *Noah*

demonstrate an enduring fascination with the drama and the passion to be found in the stories of the Bible. Even children's toys show the influence of the Bible – the armfuls of Noah's-ark toys my children enjoy are evidence of that. One estimate suggests that over 2.5 billion copies of the Bible have been sold. This rises to 6 billion if you include the copies of the Bible that have been given away.

But approaching the Bible itself can be a bit daunting. It can be a confusing book. Go into a bookshop and find the section with Bibles and you will find quite a range of different objects all of which are the Bible. Go into a specialist Christian bookshop and you will find even more variety. There are Bibles in black leather covers, Bibles in white leather to be given as gifts, Bibles in tin boxes, in garish colours. They range in size from those too large to be held comfortably to those that will fit easily in a handbag. There are many different translations and some include a section called the 'Apocrypha' while others don't. Open a Bible and you will find small print with numbers, some large and some small. Some Bibles have certain words and phrases in red. Start to read and you will quickly find a whole host of stories, myths, genealogies, poems, hymns, letters, prophecies, visions and all kinds of material. How is anyone to make sense of this?

It can also be a scary book. It is waved by street preachers, kissed by priests and quoted by moralists. All too often the Bible is presented, by believers and atheists alike, as something at odds with many aspects of our life today. Scientific accounts of evolution are dismissed as contrary to the Bible; the Bible is seen as a place where violence is rampant, especially against those who don't belong to the Jewish or Christian faiths; and it is often cited as against marriage for gay and lesbian people (or just possibly against anyone who might find sex enjoyable). In short, the Bible is used by many, believers and atheists alike, as a book best handled only after switching off your brain.

The aim of this book is to offer a way into the Bible that respects its variety and complexity but removes some of the fear and confusion that may arise in picking up a Bible. Above all, this book arises out of the conviction that it is possible to read the Bible without switching off your brain. Indeed, I am convinced that a fully switched-on brain is essential to get the most out of the Bible. This book is an invitation, a tool kit and a guide. It is an invitation to join in the conversation about the Bible's themes and questions that begins within the Bible itself. It is a tool kit to give you some of the basic ideas, history and questions that will help you to join in those conversations. And it is a guide to some – but by no means all – of the questions those conversations address. So turn on your brain, and we will begin our exploration of this sometimes confusing but always rewarding book.

1

How to read the Bible

The Bible ... is a book that has been read more, and
examined less, than any book that ever existed.

Thomas Paine[1]

Open up the Bible and you will find a talking snake, people living
for hundreds of years, giants walking the earth, an elderly couple
moving to live in a strange land, angels sitting down at table, a woman
turning into salt, a man trying to sacrifice his own son, marriages
on the basis of who a servant met at a well, a father who can't tell
the difference between his sons, a man tricked into marrying the
elder sister of his intended, flocks of sheep that bore speckled and
striped fleeces, and a slave falsely convicted of rape who becomes
the second most powerful man in the kingdom. Through all of this,
God is present. God speaks, gets angry, sends floods, protects people,
makes promises, calls people to abandon all that they know, wrestles
with a man through the night and guides his chosen people. And
that is just the first book of the Bible!

The Bible is a strange book – it is supposed to be. There are things
in it that date back thousands of years. There are things that speak
of odd and difficult experiences. It is all right to find the Bible strange,
difficult or odd. It is also a book that can speak powerfully to us.
Because it is strange it can come into our world in an angular way
and disrupt our normal patterns of looking and give us something
new, something to learn. The Bible needs to be strange because it is
trying to point beyond human experience to God, and God is not
part of our world. Perhaps it is only through the strange, surprising
and puzzling that we can be told something about God.

Chapter and verse

Before we begin to look at how to read this strange and fascinating book we need to look at the numbers you will find in the margin or through the text of almost all Bibles. Each book of the Bible has been divided into chapters and verses in order to make it easier to navigate. The convention is to write the name of a book, a chapter and then a verse so that the reader can find things from larger divisions to small ones. So if I were to write 'John 11.35', to find this you would look at the Gospel of John. Then you would find chapter 11 and then verse 35. It reads 'Jesus began to weep' or in some translations 'Jesus wept'. It is the shortest verse in the Bible.

These divisions are very helpful, and a chapter is usually a chunk that it makes sense to read together. Some care needs to be taken when reading, however, as the chapters and verses were not something the biblical writers included. They were added later. Chapters were added by a thirteenth-century Archbishop of Canterbury, Stephen Langton (1150–1228). Verses had to wait until the sixteenth century, when the system devised in 1551 by Robert Estienne, a French printer, was adopted. Just occasionally the chapter divisions of the Bible cut across the sense of a longer argument and may skew our understanding.

How not to read the Bible

The obvious way to read the Bible, and the downfall of many, would seem to be to pick it up, start on page one and finish at the end. That is how we normally approach a book. However, doing this will mean that you will struggle to reach the end of the book of Genesis (the first book of the Bible). If you make it through that you will almost certainly fail to finish the book of Leviticus (the third book). It is important to remember that the Bible is a library, and as such we can choose books from different places. There are books we wouldn't dream of reading cover to cover, such as textbooks and telephone directories. There are particular ways of making sense of these books, suited to the sort of book they are. The Bible also has ways of reading that are particular to itself. Beginning at page one is not one of them. I have nothing against the discipline of reading through the whole Bible – perhaps it is something every Bible reader should do at least once in their life. But it should not be the normal way.

Another way of engaging with the Bible to avoid is the 'lucky dip' approach, opening it at random and reading whatever you find. There is a cautionary tale of a man who opened his Bible and stuck a pin in the page to find the verse he would take as his reading for the day. One day he did this and the pin landed on Matthew 27.5. This tells of Judas despairing at having betrayed Jesus and says: 'Throwing down the pieces of silver in the Temple, he departed; and he went and hanged himself.' Not finding this a great inspiration for the day ahead, the man tried again. This time the pin landed on Luke 10.37, the end of the parable of the Good Samaritan, 'Jesus said to him, "Go and do likewise."' Getting worried now, the man tried once more. This time the pin landed on John 13.27, and he read 'Jesus said to him, "Do quickly what you are going to do."' This story is a warning against using the Bible as a fortune teller. It is not a magic book, providing the right words at random. It is a book that embodies a conversation about God and his people. Random snippets of conversation rarely enlighten us but are very good at leading to misunderstandings!

None of this is to deny that at times particular verses stand out and seem to say something very particular and pertinent to us in the situations in which we find ourselves. Many Bible readers will attest to having been surprised and challenged, guided and helped by particular words or phrases. One great example is Dietrich Bonhoeffer, the German Lutheran pastor executed in 1945 for his part in a plot to assassinate Hitler. In June 1939 Bonhoeffer was in America. As war came closer his friends there and in Germany were telling him to remain in the United States for his own safety. Bonhoeffer, however, was reading the Bible – his diary for the month includes repeated mention of daily readings. The entry for 26 June says:

> Today, by chance, I read II Tim. 4.21, 'Do your best to come
> before winter' – Paul's request to Timothy. Timothy is to share

the suffering of the Apostle and not to be ashamed. 'Do your best to come before winter' – otherwise it might be too late. That has been in my ears all day . . . 'Do your best to come before winter' – it is not a misuse of Scripture if I take that to be said to me.[2]

Bonhoeffer decided to return to Germany and to play his part in resisting the Nazi government. Clearly this verse, which Bonhoeffer took 'to be said to me', played an important part in confirming this decision, a chance reading that had this influence on him. Here we can see the power of particular parts of the Bible in saying important things to people. But it is not a random or a fortune-telling approach. Rather, Bonhoeffer read this verse in its own context and in his own context. Context is an important feature of good Bible reading, and it is worth spending some time examining how.

Context: Who? Where? When? Why?

When Bonhoeffer chanced upon that verse he didn't simply take it as instruction, he also sees the context in which it was written. Paul is in prison, suffering. He has been deserted by his companions and longs for Timothy to come to him. All of this context is understood by Bonhoeffer as he reads that single verse. The context of isolation, suffering and longing come from the context of the writer. This enriches how Bonhoeffer can read it in his own context of the United States in 1939.

Reading his diaries is an insight into Bonhoeffer's context. War is brewing in Europe and he is in America, safe but distant from those he loves and the fight against Hitler. His diary entries for the days around 26 June, when he read that verse, record his struggles with being in the United States and not knowing where to go. In fact he made the decision to return home on 20 June, but the tone of his entries changes after reading this verse from 2 Timothy. He stops agonizing about his decision and is more resolute in making plans for returning to Germany. Bonhoeffer's context resonates with that of the verse from the Bible. He feels isolated, detached and knows that to return to Germany will lead to suffering. It is not an exact match, but awareness of both contexts makes for a much deeper and richer understanding of the Bible verse.

There are different contexts, then, for Bonhoeffer's understanding of this verse – three in particular stand out. First there is the context in which the verse is written. Paul is in prison, and historians can tell us something about the conditions in which he might have been held. Second there is the context of the verse within the Bible and the book of the Bible (2 Timothy). It is part of the closing greetings of a letter, and there we learn of Paul being deserted and his longing for Timothy to be with him. Third there is the context in which Bonhoeffer reads the verse. Isolated and having decided to return to Germany, he finds much that speaks to his situation. He reads it in the light of the decision he has made and the likely consequences.

These contexts can also help us as we read the Bible. The more we know about each of these contexts, the better our understanding of the Bible passage will be. In terms of the first context (the context in which the Bible passage is written), here are some good questions to ask:

- Who wrote this, to whom and why?
- Where and when were they writing?

In terms of the second context (the context of the passage within the book and within the whole Bible), these are useful questions to ask:

- What sort of literature is this?
- How does this passage fit into the rest of the book and the whole of the Bible?

Not all of these questions can be answered in relation to every passage or book of the Bible. We don't always know who wrote the books of the Bible or when or where they wrote them. Scholars may have speculated, often very convincingly, though that is far from certainty. But ask the questions you can, look around the passage and see where it is coming from and where it is going. That can make a huge difference to our understanding.

But equally important is looking at the third context (the context in which we read the Bible). I am a man, a husband and a father;

I work for the Church; I live in a Derbyshire village; I have far more than the global average income. All of these, and more, affect the way I read the Bible and the presuppositions I bring to any passage from it. This is not to say that I need to change any of these factors in my life (although I may), but simply that each has an influence. The more I understand my own context and the better I understand myself, the more I will understand why I read the Bible in the way I do. Some good questions to ask might be:

- Whom do I naturally identify with in this passage?
- Are there things I find it hard to see because of where I read this from?

Reading the Bible well involves understanding something of how the Bible came to be; of what the Bible is; of who we are as readers. Bringing all of that together helps us to read the Bible well.

Ten 'commandments' for Bible reading

As well as attention to these three contexts, I want to offer ten ways of reading that will help us read the Bible well. They are all practical. Good Bible readers will use all of them at different times.

1 Pray

The Bible invites us to be part of a conversation about God and about God's people. Even the book of Esther, which doesn't mention God, is about God and his people. Praying, asking God to help us as we read, is simply about asking that we might join the conversation and see things that will help us understand our place in the conversation. If you are not a Christian you may choose not to pray, or you may decide that a prayer can't hurt and pray anyway. Whether you are a believer or not, starting with prayer can help us to be surprised by what we find when we read. I recommend it. It won't make you a professor of biblical studies overnight but it might help you to be open to something you hadn't seen in the Bible before. In Chapter 6 we will look more closely at the interaction between the Bible and prayer. For now, let me suggest a prayer that might be useful before reading the Bible.

God of all knowledge,
help me now as I read from the Bible.
May I be surprised by what I read,
guided in where it takes me
and helped in my understanding.
I make this prayer in the name of Jesus Christ,
your living Word. Amen.

2 Find a good translation

The chances are that you will read the Bible in English; that is to say, in translation. One of the most important features of the Bible is that it is translatable, that it remains the Bible even when translated into another language. This is one of the key differences between the way Christians read the Bible and the way Muslims read the Qur'an which, to be the inspired and holy book, must be read in Arabic – the language in which it was originally written.

And yet there are a large number of English translations, which complicates the whole business of choosing a Bible to use regularly. How do we find a translation with which we feel comfortable? I do not think there is any real need to worry about the accuracy of translation. Most Bible translations embody a huge amount of genuine care and attention to detail. The differences between them are mostly minor, and when they are more significant things just get more interesting – that's when things come alive. (It's also a good reason to read with others – see commandment 8!)

If you go to church regularly you may want to read at home the version of the Bible used at your church or something different for variety. Either way you need to find out what version is used in the church you attend. Other than that, I suggest you simply find one that seems to work for you.

As a help, let me suggest some key features of five different translations.

The Authorized Version (AV), also called the King James Version (KJV)

For many years this was the only English version of the Bible readily available. It is the most poetic of the English Bibles. Some people find that the AV's language trips off the tongue; it is the language they hear when the Bible is read aloud. However, it was translated before we had access to some of the best and earliest manuscripts and does suffer a little from inaccuracy. It also feels very distant and alien to many – this is not the English we regularly speak. I wouldn't recommend the AV to a new reader of the Bible, but if this is the version that works for you, then use it!

THE MESSAGE

At the other end of the spectrum, THE MESSAGE is a very contemporary translation into English as it is spoken today. It is the work of a single translator, which makes it consistent in style. It is fresh and sometimes really makes a passage come alive. The downside is that the language is so contemporary that it will date quickly. Readers outside the United States may also find it overly American.

The New International Version (NIV)

This translation comes from an Evangelical Protestant background. It was the first version I used for regular Bible reading. It has a contemporary feel and is widely available in lots of different forms. The NIV is regularly updated and regards these changes as an important part of its mission.

The New Jerusalem Bible (NJB)

This version comes from a Roman Catholic background. It also has a contemporary feel and – other than the Authorized Version – is probably the best at communicating poetry in the Bible.

The New Revised Standard Version (NRSV)

This is the version of the Bible that I have chosen to use for quotations in this book. It is widely used by churches. It stands in the traditions of the Authorized Version but has used the best manuscripts of the Bible that we have in preparing a translation. It has also sensitively used inclusive language for men and women. A tried and tested translation.

None of these translations is perfect, but any of them will enable you to read the Bible in English, as will the many other translations available. Finding one that helps you is a matter of personal taste. Let me make two further suggestions. First, borrow one from a friend, from a church, from the library, and 'test-drive' it for a month or so. If it works for you, use that version. Otherwise try another. Second, go to a Christian bookshop, a shop that specializes in selling Bibles and other religious literature. The staff there will be delighted to help you choose a Bible that suits you, and are knowledgeable about the range of translations available.

3 Read in small bits

The Bible is not a book to read easily from cover to cover, so read a small bit of it, a passage. Don't feel you have to read the whole Bible tomorrow. Read a bit, see what you make of it, see what it makes of you. Then read another bit another day. Dipping into the books of the Bible or reading a book by reading a small part each day or week are very good ways of reading the Bible.

There are resources to help you do this. Many churches will use something called a lectionary, which is simply a plan for reading. A lectionary is a helpful tool, and using one means that the church doesn't just read until the reader gets bored and gives up. Using a lectionary ensures I am not simply reading the parts of the Bible I like but that I read the difficult and challenging parts as well. The official church lectionary might not be the best place to start Bible reading, but there are many other schemes for reading the Bible in smaller sections. You could even devise your own. Why not simply pick a book and read a chapter at a time?

The Bible is not a book to be understood overnight. It is a book that will feed you and speak to you day by day over years. Reading it in small bits is to be swept up in the great river of the Bible. You won't understand it all but will come to understand more and more as you read it regularly. Read and reread it. You will find new things in passages you thought you knew really well.

4 Read in large chunks

Showering regularly is a good way to stay clean, but nothing beats a lengthy soak in a good hot bath. In a similar way, if reading in small bits is the normal way of reading the Bible, it is good from time to time to read it in larger chunks. Read a whole book or a section of a book. Let the story wash over you and get to know it in outline.

Reading only in small bits can leave us knowing those bits very well but not really how they join up. To do that we need to read in larger bits. In Mark's Gospel, for example, everything seems to happen 'immediately', but you wouldn't spot that if you only read one passage – it can only be seen by reading Mark as a whole or in larger chunks. Why not start by reading through a whole Gospel? Mark is only 16 chapters long and can be read in a few hours. Set aside some time and enjoy immersing yourself in a whole Gospel.

5 Read aloud

The Bible was not written for the way we read today. It was written for cultures in which few people could read and before the advent of printing. The Bible was written to be read aloud. Even the most intimate of Paul's letters would have been spoken out loud to its first audience. Reading the Bible aloud is to join in with this tradition and to hear the Bible as it was intended to be heard. If you hear the Bible in church it is most likely to be read aloud. Whether the church knows it or not, it is joining in a very ancient tradition of reading that goes right back to the origins of the Bible.

Reading aloud also slows us down and helps us to notice more. Things sound different when spoken and heard rather than read silently from the page. The closer attention this requires of us is helpful in approaching any text, and especially so in the case of the Bible. It works for short passages and for long ones. Read a short passage aloud to yourself – notice the difference it makes, how the text speaks as you give it voice.

6 Get to know the stories

The Bible is full of stories, and many parts of it have echoes of other stories. To read the Bible well it is good to know the stories. A friend of mine who studied Greek and Latin literature at university was advised to read a collection of children's versions of the myths before he got to university. 'We can teach you the rest,' his tutor told him, 'but you need to know the stories.' The same is true with the Bible: get to know the stories. Reading a children's Bible – and there are several that tell the stories well – is a good place to start doing this. My favourites are *The Lion First Bible* and *The Lion Storyteller Bible*,[3] though you or a child you know may have your own favourite.

7 See how the Bible reads itself

Because the Bible was written over many years, its writers often knew earlier parts before they wrote. This means that the Bible often reads itself, and often in interesting ways. One example – which did much to inspire me to write this book – is from Mark 12.28–30:

> One of the scribes came near and heard them disputing with one another, and seeing that he answered them well, he asked him, 'Which commandment is the first of all?' Jesus answered, 'The first is, "Hear, O Israel: the Lord our God, the Lord is one; you shall love the Lord your God with all your heart, and with all your soul, and with all your mind, and with all your strength."'

Here Jesus quotes Deuteronomy 6.4–5: 'Hear, O Israel: The Lord is our God, the Lord alone. You shall love the Lord your God with all your heart, and with all your soul, and with all your might.' The difference is clear. Jesus adds 'mind' to the list of things that the commandment says we are to use to love God; Deuteronomy makes no reference to 'mind' at all. Much scholarly attention has been paid to this, and in fact Jesus has combined two variant readings of the Greek translation of the Old Testament, one of which substitutes 'mind' for 'heart'. But we get something of an insight into how Jesus reads the Bible. He adds to it, looking for a comprehensive way of living it. He does not read it absolutely word for word but regards the Bible as a living thing he can interpret by adding things together. So watch for how the Bible reads itself. It does so in all kinds of ways – look for them.

8 Read with other people

The Bible was never addressed to individuals. Even the letters that seem to be written to named people were probably read aloud to groups. The Bible is meant to be read and discussed together. That is why churches read it when they gather together for worship. But discussion groups, reading groups or just groups of friends and neighbours reading it together are also an important part of reading the Bible.

As well as that, read with the great Bible readers of history. The Bible has thousands of years of interpretation. This is a conversation about the conversation that the Bible has about God and his people. Entering this conversation about the conversation can be a fascinating and a helpful resource for Bible readers today. A good way of doing this is to use a commentary. There are commentaries on every book of the Bible. The For Everyone series of commentaries, written by Tom Wright and John Goldingay and published by SPCK, are very helpful ways into the books of the Bible. Eugene Peterson, who produced THE MESSAGE translation of the Bible, says that 'reading commentaries has always seemed to me analogous to the gathering of football fans in the local bar after the game, replaying in endless detail the game they have just watched.'[4]

Reading with others, whether in person, through history or with commentaries, is a really helpful way of reading the Bible. Why not find a Bible-reading group or set one up? Or find a commentary on a book of the Bible and enter the conversation about the conversation.

9 Be prepared to be changed

The point of reading the Bible – and arguably the point of reading anything – is to be changed. In fact it is the point of being alive. There is no point in being alive if you are not prepared to change – you might as well be a stone (and even then you will change, just very slowly). To read the Bible is to open ourselves up to being changed. So read it and be prepared for it to challenge you, to change you – that is what it is there for.

10 Wrestle

The Bible contains an important story about Jacob and about how he came to be called Israel, after whom God's people were named. Jacob was a trickster, a liar and a cheat. He ran away from his brother, having tricked him out of his inheritance and out of their father's blessing. He returned home having become rich but was understandably nervous about meeting his brother again. The Bible tells this story of an encounter with a strange man on the night before he did:

The same night he got up and took his two wives, his two maids, and his eleven children, and crossed the ford of the Jabbok. He took them and sent them across the stream, and likewise everything that he had. Jacob was left alone; and a man wrestled with him until daybreak. When the man saw that he did not prevail against Jacob, he struck him on the hip socket; and Jacob's hip was put out of joint as he wrestled with him. Then he said, 'Let me go, for the day is breaking.' But Jacob said, 'I will not let you go, unless you bless me.' So he said to him, 'What is your name?' And he said, 'Jacob.' Then the man said, 'You shall no longer be called Jacob, but Israel, for you have striven with God and with humans, and have prevailed.' Then Jacob asked him, 'Please tell me your name.' But he said, 'Why is it that you ask my name?' And there he blessed him. So Jacob called the place Peniel, saying, 'For I have seen God face to face, and yet my life is preserved.' The sun rose upon him as he passed Penuel, limping because of his hip. Therefore to this day the Israelites do not eat the thigh muscle that is on the hip socket, because he struck Jacob on the hip socket at the thigh muscle. (Genesis 32.22–32)

Jacob wrestles with a man who turns out to be God. He is changed by the encounter, receiving both a new name and a limp. The name is very important: 'Israel' means 'one who strives with God'. God calls his whole people to wrestle with him. It is not an easy relationship but one that takes effort and can feel like fighting. The Bible is not a diktat from on high or an email from heaven. It is a conversation, and not an easy one. It can even turn into a wrestling match.

For us who read the Bible, then, this means that we are allowed to find it difficult. We are even allowed to be outraged by it. What is important, in the first place, is to be honest about how it makes us feel. Some parts will appal us and make us feel that God needs to change. That's all right – be appalled. But hold on and wrestle until you find something more.

Some years ago a publisher produced a series of individual books of the Bible with prefaces by famous authors. Louis de Bernières wrote the introduction to the book of Job, in which he described God as 'an unpleasantly sarcastic megalomaniac'.[5] This provoked a letter of complaint sent to every clergy person in the Church of England. However, if you only read the book of Job you might come to the conclusion that de Bernières had it right. But Job isn't the only book in the Bible.

We are to wrestle with the Bible. It isn't always easy. We need to be honest about what we think about what we read. That might not be where we leave it but it is a necessary first step. We must not on any account be too pious in our Bible reading; the Bible is many things but pious it is not. Jacob is presented as the cheat and liar he was; David the great king is an adulterer and a murderer. The Bible is quite honest about its heroes. There may be hope for the rest of us.

The eleventh commandment – read it!

There is always an eleventh commandment! And this one is simple: read the Bible. Many people pontificate about the Bible but one wonders if they actually read it regularly. The Bible is full of interest and can be a lifelong passion, but it needs to be read. Commentaries and books about the Bible – including this one – are only useful if they help us read the Bible itself. Read it.

Try it out

1 Go to a Christian bookshop and ask them to help you find a translation of the Bible that works for you.
2 Get together with some friends and arrange to read a book of the Bible together. I suggest starting with Mark's Gospel.
3 Read it!

Further reading

Tom Wright, *Mark for Everyone*, London: SPCK, 2001.
John Goldingay, *Genesis for Everyone*, 2 vols, London: SPCK, 2010.

2

What is the Bible?

---•◦•---

The Greek *Biblia* is in the plural ... it reminds us that there
are many voices to be heard within the Bible.

Diarmaid MacCulloch[1]

How about a quiz? It's a very simple one: are the following statements
true or false?

1 The Bible is the most translated book in history.
2 Two books of the Bible don't mention God.
3 The Bible is the most shoplifted book in the world.
4 Some versions of the Bible have 66 books, some 73 books and
  some 81 books.
5 The Bible is clear to understand and no one has ever argued about
  its meaning.

The answer is that they are all true – apart from the last one.

First, the Bible is indeed the most translated book in history.
There are translations of at least one book of the Bible in 2,590 languages, and 495 languages have the complete Bible. This does not
count the numerous translations of the Bible in English, something
we looked at in Chapter 1; on my shelves I have at least 16 different
English translations. There is even a version of the Bible in Klingon –
search online if you don't believe me. Second, neither Esther (in
Hebrew) nor the Song of Songs mention God. Third, it is widely re-
ported that the Bible is the most shoplifted book in the world – I don't
think this includes those taken from churches or hotel rooms. Fourth,
depending upon which Christian tradition has produced the Bible,
it will contain 66 books (Protestant), 73 books (Roman Catholic)
or more. The Ethiopian Coptic Church has 81 books in its Bible. All
share, however, the core 66 texts. Fifth, there has never been a time

in Jewish or Christian history when the Bible hasn't provoked arguments between readers. All of this means that it is important to look a little more closely at the Bible. What precisely is this book?

One book or many?

The first thing to notice is that the Bible is not one single book but a collection of many. Have you ever written a story by writing a couple of sentences on paper, folding it over to hide what you have written and then passing it on? After several people have contributed their sentences the result is a mixture of styles, subjects and material. The Bible can feel like this. It was written by many different authors; most did not know the others; nor that their writing would be collected with the other books. The result is that the Bible speaks with a range of voices. It presents us with a mixture of material that sometimes does not fit easily together.

The word 'Bible' comes from the Greek word *biblia*, which means 'books' or 'library'. The Greek word is plural, and this plural noun survived into use in Latin. However, over the course of time it was used as a singular noun. By the time modern European languages developed, this was the form it took. Hence the English form, 'the Bible', is singular. All of this was probably compounded by the arrival of the printing press, which enabled the production of a single volume containing all of the books of the Bible.

As well as different books written by different authors, the Bible contains many different genres. Within the 66 core books you can find myth, history, legal codes, prayers, poetry, letters, prophecy, visions and more. It is important to be aware of the genre of what we are reading, otherwise we might completely miss the point. George Orwell's 1945 novel *Animal Farm* is not simply a story about talking animals and unpleasant pigs on a farm, it is an allegory for the Russian revolution of 1917 and its aftermath. Not to understand the allegorical and satirical genre of the novel is to miss its point completely. In the case of the Bible, understanding the genre of its different parts is equally important.

The Bible is a collection of huge diversity, which is one of its most important features. It is not a single voice, it is a conversation. Some of the voices seem to speak about very different things; others seem to argue with earlier speakers. This conversation draws us in, invites us to take part. It is a conversation about God, and each different voice offers a different set of insights into God. All of them are needed to fill out the picture of God the Bible offers.

Some writers on leadership speak about 'wicked problems', problems that are complex and difficult to solve because the information about them seems to be changing or contradictory. Indeed, the definition of such a problem is not agreed by those confronted by it, let alone the shape of the solution. The term 'wicked' in relation to such problems means 'intensely difficult' rather than evil. A wicked problem is unique, new and has no obvious way through it. The role of the leader in confronting a wicked problem is not to run in and offer a solution, it is to allow the whole range of questions to come to the surface so that all the different aspects of the problem are seen. As many voices as possible need to be heard. It seems to me that God is a wicked problem. God is not easy to get hold of, and there are different and contradictory approaches to God. The many voices of the Bible enable us to get as wide a picture of God as possible, and they invite us to join our voices to addressing the questions that arise when considering God.

Which books are included in the Bible?

All Christian Bibles contain a core of 66 books. They are divided into two sections or Testaments – a word that means 'promise'. The Old Testament collects books based around the promise of God to his chosen people, the Jews. There are 39 core books in the Old Testament:

- Genesis, Exodus, Leviticus, Numbers, Deuteronomy (the Torah or Law);
- Joshua, Judges, Ruth, 1 and 2 Samuel, 1 and 2 Kings, 1 and 2 Chronicles, Ezra, Nehemiah, Esther (the Histories);
- Job, Psalms, Proverbs, Ecclesiastes, Song of Songs (the Wisdom writings);
- Isaiah, Jeremiah, Lamentations, Ezekiel, Daniel (the Major Prophets);
- Hosea, Joel, Amos, Obadiah, Jonah, Micah, Nahum, Habakkuk, Zephaniah, Haggai, Zechariah, Malachi (the Minor Prophets).

The New Testament collects books written around the promise of God to people of every nation in Jesus. It has 27 core books:

- Matthew, Mark, Luke, John (the Gospels);
- The Acts of the Apostles (a history of the early Church);
- Romans, 1 and 2 Corinthians, Galatians, Ephesians, Philippians, Colossians, 1 and 2 Thessalonians, 1 and 2 Timothy, Titus, Philemon (the letters of Paul);
- Hebrews, James, 1 and 2 Peter, 1, 2 and 3 John, Jude (the catholic or general letters);
- Revelation (a vision).

Many Bibles, however, also contain a third section called the Apocrypha. This is a set of extra books and some additions to existing books (Esther and Daniel). The Apocrypha is not an extra testament. It collects books that are added to the Old Testament in some but not all Christian traditions. Many Bibles print them in between the Old and New Testaments. Most of the books of the Apocrypha are found in the authoritative Greek translation of the Old Testament from the second century BC. This is called the Septuagint – which means 'seventy' – because according to legend, 72 scholars, six from each tribe of Israel, were placed in 72 separate rooms and each produced an identical translation of the Bible. The Septuagint is the version of the Old Testament most often quoted in the New Testament.

There is a great deal of interesting material in the Apocrypha, and in its additions the book of Esther does mention God! But the Greek books have not been accepted into Jewish Bibles since the second or third century AD. It was not really until the sixteenth century that Christians began to question their inclusion. That was largely a response to the upheaval in the Church known as the Reformation. Protestants, finding that Catholic doctrines and practices – not least praying for the dead – were supported by passages from the books only found in the Septuagint, rejected those books and accepted only the Hebrew books of the Old Testament. This was supported by the observation that the books of the Apocrypha are not quoted in the New Testament. Various Protestant confessions and statements of faith list the books of the Bible so as to exclude the Greek books. Catholics, finding that the Greek books supported their position, listed the books to include them. The Church of England, ever looking for a middle position, suggests the Apocrypha be read 'for example of life and instruction of manners' but not in order to 'establish any doctrine' (Article 6 of the 39 Articles).

Other Christian traditions, especially the Ethiopian Coptic Church, have included an even wider selection of books within the Bible. But all traditions agree on the 66 core texts – the 39 Hebrew books of the Old Testament and the 27 books of the New Testament. It is these books that I shall focus on in the remainder of this book.

How did the Old Testament come together?

There is an ongoing argument among Doctor Who fans about which stories should be counted as official. As well as the television stories there are many Doctor Who stories in novels, comics and audio plays. Whether these stories are part of the official story of the Doctor is a question fans debate at great length. And the question they ask is: 'Are these part of the canon?' Exactly the same question is asked about books of the Bible.

The word 'canon' means a rule. To ask if a book of the Bible (or a Doctor Who story) is in the canon means to ask if the rule includes it. The canon of the Bible is simply the list of the books included in the Bible. It was written later than the Bible. Within the Bible we can find glimpses of how the canon formed and how it might have been different.

The Old Testament canon was a cause of argument among the different parties within Judaism at the time of Jesus. We can see this in the Gospels. The Pharisees accepted all of the books of what Christians now call the Old Testament; the Sadducees only accepted the Torah. These differences vanished as Rabbinic Judaism grew up in the first and second centuries after Jesus. The Jewish list of books contains only the 39 core books of the Old Testament. Naturally they don't call it the Old Testament, and the books are in a different order.

The New Testament itself offers a couple of intriguing examples of alternative paths that could have been chosen. The letter of Jude records that:

Enoch, in the seventh generation from Adam, prophesied, saying, 'See, the Lord is coming with tens of thousands of his holy
ones, to execute judgement on all, and to convict everyone of
all the deeds of ungodliness that they have committed in such
an ungodly way, and of all the harsh things that ungodly sinners
have spoken against him.'   (Jude 14–15)

This quotes the first book of Enoch, a book of visions and dreams
written between 300 BC and AD 100. Yet this book is not even in the
Apocrypha. Only the Ethiopian and Eritrean Orthodox Churches
regard 1 Enoch as part of the Bible.

A further puzzle can be found in Matthew's Gospel. As part of
the story of Jesus' birth and childhood, Matthew writes that 'he
made his home in a town called Nazareth, so that what had been
spoken through the prophets might be fulfilled, "He shall be called
a Nazorean"' (Matthew 2.23). This follows a pattern of stories demon-
strating the fulfilment of particular passages of the Old Testament
that recurs throughout the first two chapters of Matthew's Gospel.
But despite the best efforts of many scholars, the quotation has never
been identified. Quite which prophecy Matthew thought was being
fulfilled is unknown.

But these are about the only two exceptions to a lengthy but largely
very smooth process of devising the canon of the Old Testament,
the list of accepted books. The only real argument came in the sixteenth century when, as we have seen, Protestant Christians stopped
reading the Greek books (the Apocrypha). Jewish lists had omitted
these books since the second century after Jesus.

How did books get into the New Testament?

The list of books accepted into the New Testament took less time
and has more bumps on the way. To begin with the early Christians
read the Old Testament as their Bible. They probably also told stories
of Jesus, handed on from the first disciples. As the first disciples came
to die, towards the end of the first century after Jesus, these stories
were written and collected into the Gospels. In addition, the leaders
of the Church wrote letters to congregations. These letters were

also kept and read again and again. The letters written by Paul are the largest collection preserved, and are referred to in the second letter of Peter – evidence that they were regarded as important from a very early time, although Peter does warn that 'There are some things in them hard to understand' (2 Peter 3.15–16).

The production of a list of accepted New Testament books began in the second century. This first list is known as Marcion's Canon. Marcion was the name of the writer of the list, and his canon included only ten of St Paul's letters and a heavily edited version of Luke's Gospel. Marcion saw Christianity as an entirely separate religion from Judaism, and his canon rules out all of the Old Testament, together with large chunks of the New, those which he considered too Jewish. Marcion's canon was rejected by the Church as a whole but one of its lasting effects was that new lists were written and the question of which books were to be included in the Bible was opened.

Other than Marcion's list, most of the canons make no reference to the books of the Old Testament. Agreement on these is simply assumed. But in different places the list of books used to make up the New Testament varied. Some books, such as the four Gospels, the Acts of the Apostles and Paul's letters to the Romans and Corinthians, were common to all of the lists. Others, such as the book of Revelation, the Shepherd of Hermas and the letter of Barnabas, feature on some of the earliest lists but not on all. Of these three, only Revelation made it into the final lists of the books accepted as part of the Bible. But both the Shepherd of Hermas and the letter of Barnabas have been found attached to early Christian copies of the Bible as a sort of appendix. By the mid-fourth century the list of 27 books that we know as the New Testament seems to have come together. It took a little over 200 years for the process begun in reaction to Marcion to take its final form.

There have been suggestions for change since then. The German reformer Martin Luther wanted to exclude Hebrews, James (which he described as 'an epistle of straw'[2]), Jude and Revelation from the New Testament. This was never accepted, and Luther included them when he translated the New Testament into German. To this day, however, these four books are put together at the back of German

Lutheran Bibles. Once fixed, the list of the 27 books of the New Testament has not changed.

Could we add a book to the Bible?

Imagine the scene at a press conference. There has been some archaeological digging in the desert of Egypt and a previously unknown letter has been discovered. It claims to have been written by Paul. At the press conference the archaeologist reveals a mass of evidence. There is carbon dating, accounts of first-century trade routes, theological parallels with the letters we do have and overlaps in the literary style. All suggest that this really is a letter written by Paul. The newspaper headlines are quick to suggest that a new book of the Bible has been found. But they beg the question of whether such a discovery would be added to the Bible.

There are in fact at least two potential candidates for such a letter. In what we have as the first letter of Paul to the Corinthians, Paul writes that 'I wrote to you in my letter not to associate with sexually immoral persons' (1 Corinthians 5.9), which suggests that Paul had already written a letter to Corinth. And in his letter to the Colossians, Paul urges them to 'see that you read also the letter from Laodicea' (Colossians 4.16). Might this mean that there is a 3 Corinthians (or a 0 Corinthians, since it would precede 1 Corinthians) and a letter to the Laodiceans out there somewhere, awaiting an archaeological discovery? Many scholars think that the Corinthian letter is actually edited into the letters we already have, and that the Laodicean letter is in fact the letter to the Ephesians. But these are not universally held opinions, and they could be wrong.

So imagine a second press conference. This one is given by the leaders of the churches, responding to the new finding. Without disputing the authenticity of the letter they are much cooler about it than the newspaper headlines. Some are excited by the new find, others more reserved – but none are rushing to add the new letter to the canon of the Bible. Some are dogmatic – the list is closed, they say. If we had been meant to have this new letter it would have been preserved with the others. Others are more open – it takes time, they suggest, to see if this really belongs with the other letters.

My own view is this: if a 'new' letter from Paul were really uncovered, I think there would be quite a fanfare about the discovery. There would be a lot of academic argument about authenticity or otherwise. It would be printed and sell moderately well, simply out of interest. If the letter turned out to be rather banal (simply Paul listing things he'd like sent to him), it would become the preserve of scholars and find its place in the footnotes to learned articles. If, however, it had a passage of really inspirational writing, people might start to cite that alongside existing passages of Paul. Over time it might be printed as an appendix or an extra feature of Bibles. Over a couple of generations it could find its way into the body of the Bible. This would only happen, I think, if the newly discovered letter were used as part of the worship and teaching of the Church. The existing canons of the Bible took centuries to form – some of that time was needed to test the books' value in the worship and life of the Jewish and Christian communities. That time and that work would also have to be put into assessing a new letter. And, of course, there would be many arguments along the way! There would remain some who did not accept the new letter, which in turn would have an effect on the way it was used. These arguments reflect how important the Bible is to Christians – and that is the final thing we have to look at in this chapter.

Why is the Bible important?

The Bible makes claims about itself and its nature. 'All scripture is inspired by God and is useful for teaching, for reproof, for correction, and for training in righteousness, so that everyone who belongs to God may be proficient, equipped for every good work' (2 Timothy 3.16–17). The Bible is important, at least by its own claim, because it is inspired – it comes from God. The Bible is also important because it is useful for teaching, correction and training – it shapes the lives of Christians. These are two reasons why the Bible is important for Christians – it comes from God and it shapes our lives.

Once again, to say that the Bible comes from God does not mean that it is an easy book, smooth and consistent. Any account of its importance that tries to make it out as such is quite plainly wrong.

It is many books, containing different voices that don't always agree. When this passage from 2 Timothy speaks of the Bible as 'inspired', it uses the word used to translate the Hebrew word used in the book of Genesis when God 'breathed' into the dust and created the first human being (Genesis 2.7). 'Inspired' in English is simply a reference to breathing. To say the Bible is inspired is not to deny that it is a human book – quite the opposite. If the Bible is breathed by God then it is just like we human beings. Like us it is given life by God. It was written by people, just as we were born from people. The claim that the Bible is inspired is the claim that it contains life and that this life is a gift from God.

The second claim that the Bible makes about itself is that it shapes our lives. Christians use the Bible, as 2 Timothy suggests, to teach, to tell us where we are going wrong and to correct us, and to train us in doing what is right. All of the various voices in the Bible contribute to this. In doing so they point beyond the Bible to God and to Jesus. The Bible points beyond itself. In stories and letters, poems and prayers, it speaks of God and of Jesus. Living with the Bible, reading and chewing over what it says, is a way of living in the presence of God.

Christians regularly speak of the Bible as the 'Word of God' and as an authority. Yet these are most properly terms used of Jesus. In John's Gospel, Jesus is described as the 'Word of God', present at creation and structuring the world, then becoming flesh and living among us in order to set all things right (John 1.1–14). The pattern of living among, dying and rising to new life that is the story of Jesus is the pattern through which the Bible is to be read.

At the end of Matthew's Gospel, Jesus says that 'All authority in heaven and on earth has been given to me' (Matthew 28.18). Jesus is the authority to which the Bible's authority points. Paul describes how Jesus humbled himself and became human, and accepted death on a cross. Because of this God exalted him so that every knee should bow to his name (Philippians 2.5–11). Again, the pattern of Jesus becoming human, dying and being raised is the pattern of authority to which the Bible points.

The Bible shapes our lives but it shapes them into the pattern of Jesus. It offers us a life, lived with people, a death in despair and then new life when all hope has vanished. This is the shape for Christian lives. The 'Word of God' is a life, not a book. All 'authority' is given to the one who lived among us, died, and was restored to new life. The pattern of the life of Jesus is what the Bible offers of itself and for its readers.

The lives of the great saints are the lives of the great Bible readers. Francis of Assisi, whose reading of the Bible led him to share the life of the poor, shows us one example of the way the authority of the Bible leads to a life lived in the shape of Jesus' life. Another example is in the way Josephine Butler found that reading the Bible took her to campaigning for the rights of prostitutes and the repeal of repressive legislation. Martin Luther King found that the Bible compelled him to stand up for the rights of his fellow black people in America, and offers yet another way the Bible shapes a life around that of Jesus.

These are but three ways the Bible exercises its authority by shaping lives. There are many more. As we read the Bible, as we join in the conversation that it contains about God, we too might find that our lives are changed and shaped in a new and different way. That is what it means for the Bible to be an authority. That is why the Bible is important for Christians.

Try it out

1 Read short passages of different genres: a prophet (Amos 5.21–24); a letter (Philemon); a prayer (Psalm 100); a Gospel (Luke 10.25–37); law (Leviticus 19.9–18); wisdom (Proverbs 11.1–6); history (1 Samuel 16.1–13).
2 Can you see the Bible shaping the lives of its readers in the Christians of the past and/or the present?

Further reading

Paula Gooder, *The Bible: A Beginner's Guide*, London: Oneworld, 2013.

Joel M. Hoffman, *The Bible's Cutting Room Floor: The Holy Scriptures Missing from Your Bible*, New York: Thomas Dunne Books, 2014.

3

The story of the Bible

'This story we find ourselves in.'
Brian D. McLaren[1]

The Bible invites us to join a conversation – a conversation about God and what it means to be part of God's people. That conversation largely takes place through the telling of stories. The Bible is a collection of stories – stories of the people of Israel, stories of Jesus, stories told by Jesus. There is a great deal of diversity in these stories, even argument, as the great conversation gets heated. But beneath all of the stories there is an overarching story that tells a story about God and his people. This is the story of the Bible – one single story. In this story there are many smaller stories, but in an important sense all of these, and the arguments and disagreements that they embody, take their place within the larger and overarching one. It is this story, the story of the whole Bible, that I hope to tell in this chapter.

The story of the Bible also tells the story of how the Bible was written. This is important. The Bible is not written from some mountain top from which the whole of the story of God and God's people can be surveyed. Rather, it is written in the midst of the story, before any definite conclusion can be seen. The story of how the Bible is written is included in the story of the Bible because the Bible belongs to God's people. God's people wrote it as a way of telling how God has been part of their lives and histories. They collected the books of the Bible, recognizing that these had something important to say in the conversation about God and his people. They continue to read the Bible as they too join in with this conversation. God's people are part of the story of the Bible, and that means you and I can also have our place within that story.

A six-act play

Tom Wright, formerly the Bishop of Durham, offers an account of the Bible as a play.

> Suppose there exists a Shakespeare play, most of whose fifth act has been lost. The first four acts provide, let us suppose, such a remarkable wealth of characterization, such a crescendo of excitement within the plot, that it is generally agreed that the play ought to be staged. Nevertheless, it is felt inappropriate actually to write a fifth act once and for all: it would freeze the play into one form, and commit Shakespeare as it were to being prospectively responsible for work not in fact his own. Better, it might be felt, to give the key parts to highly trained, sensitive and experienced Shakespearian actors, who would immerse themselves in the first four acts, and in the language of Shakespeare and his time, *and who would then be told to work out a fifth act for themselves.*[2]

Wright offers this image as a way of understanding the authority of the Bible, the first four acts of this play, and our place as improvising in the fifth act. For Wright the first four acts of the play are: creation, fall, Israel and Jesus. The writing of the New Testament is the first scene of the final act. The New Testament also contains hints of the final scene of this act – the ending of the whole play. The notion of a play is very helpful. It speaks of something greater than the text – a play has to be performed – that is not less than the text. Similarly the Bible offers a life that is to be lived. That is more than the biblical text but it is not less than the text.

I have amended Wright's account slightly so that it forms a six-act play, with the final scene of Wright's play turned into an act in itself. I have also singled out one story as being almost the whole play in miniature. Together these six acts form the story of the Bible. It is an overarching story, and one told in many different ways. Nevertheless it is one story and we have our place within it. As we examine each act in turn it will be important to ask two questions: 'What happens?' and 'Where can the story be found?' We should also note anything else of importance.

Act 1: Creation

What happens?

The first act is deceptively simple. What happens is that God creates the world. The Bible opens with the book of Genesis, the book of the beginning, and the first three words are 'In the beginning'. In Act 1, God creates the world out of nothing.

But that is not quite what happens. At the very beginning of the book of Genesis we find that the earth is 'a formless void and darkness covered the face of the deep, while the Spirit of God swept over the face of the waters' (Genesis 1.2–3[3]). We expect creation out of nothing (*ex nihilo*), and indeed this has become the orthodox Christian teaching. But it is not found much in the Bible, at least explicitly. There seems to be 'stuff' – including, at least, water – before creation happens. There is little to suggest that the doctrine of creation *ex nihilo* was a feature of biblical faith until long after most of the Old Testament had been written.

The very first reference in the Bible that can only be understood as creation *ex nihilo* comes in the second book of Maccabees, only found in the Septuagint, the Greek translation of the Old Testament and thus in the Apocrypha. It dates from the late second century BC. In the relevant passage a mother is trying to get her child to stay faithful to the God of Israel while he is being tortured to death for refusing to eat pork and refusing to give up on the Jewish law. 'I beg you, my child, to look at the heaven and the earth and see everything that is in them, and recognize that God did not make them out of things that existed' (2 Maccabees 7.28).

To be clear, most of the references to creation in the Old Testament can be read as creation *ex nihilo*. So we can read Genesis 1 with an emphasis on the 'void'. But not until 2 Maccabees does the Bible require an understanding of creation out of nothing. What is important in all of the accounts of creation, *ex nihilo* or otherwise, is that this is a deliberate act of God. It is not a mistake or an experiment. And it is good. Throughout Genesis 1 the refrain is 'God saw that it was good' (Genesis 1.4, 12, 18, 21, 25, 31). Human beings are part of this good creation – this too is an important feature of the Bible's first act.

Where is it found?

If the content of Act 1 is surprising, so is where it can be found. The story of creation is not just told in one chapter of the Bible, rather it is found throughout it. Genesis itself has two very different accounts. The first (Genesis 1.1—2.3) tells a very stylized story of creation over the course of a week. The second (Genesis 2.4–25 and continuing into the next act) tells a more intimate story of the creation of human beings in the Garden of Eden. They are two stories stuck next to one another, with different emphases, different names for God and probably different writers. They complement rather than contradict one another, shedding light on different aspects of the story of creation.

They stand with a whole host of other stories of creation, told in a number of different ways throughout the Bible. Psalm 19, which gives the composer Joseph Haydn his greatest chorus in his oratorio *The Creation*, declares that 'The heavens are telling the glory of God; and the firmament proclaims his handiwork' (Psalm 19.1). It is a hymn of praise to God and to his creation. The book of Job ends with God reminding Job of all that he has made. In particular God tells Job of Behemoth, who appears to be a great land monster, and Leviathan, a sea monster (Job 40—41). Leviathan also makes an appearance in the Psalms: 'You divided the sea by your might; you broke the heads of the dragons in the waters. You crushed the heads of Leviathan; you gave him as food for the creatures of the wilderness' (Psalm 74.13–14). He is also found in Isaiah: 'On that day the LORD . . . will punish Leviathan the fleeing serpent, Leviathan the twisting serpent, and he will kill the dragon that is in the sea' (Isaiah 27.1).

Monsters, especially sea monsters, give an important clue as to what the Bible thinks creation is primarily about. Creation for the Bible is about bringing order from chaos. That is more important for the Bible than bringing something out of nothing. Creation in the Bible is normally contrasted to chaos. Mark's Gospel tells a story about Jesus calming a storm and his disciples are petrified. 'Who then is this, that even the wind and the sea obey him?' (Mark 4.41). This is a significant story because it identifies Jesus as God, as the creator whom creation obeys. The wind and the sea are the most chaotic parts of creation, something that remains true even today. So throughout the Bible there are references to God's ability to calm the waters and to find a way of taming the sea – so much so that in the book of Revelation, in the new creation (Act 6), the sea will be no more. This is a strange thing for someone like me, who grew up at the seaside and regards the sea as something beautiful. But the sea is no more by the end of the book of Revelation (Revelation 21.1) because the sea is chaos. And when God restores creation, there will be no more chaos so there will be no more sea. I have to remind myself that the sea is a metaphor here for destructive and chaotic power!

Throughout the Bible we find references to creation. I have already suggested that stories of Jesus refer to creation. The Gospels of Matthew and John both begin with references to creation: Matthew starts 'An account of the genealogy [*genesis* in Greek] of Jesus the Messiah' (Matthew 1.1); and John with a quotation of the beginning of Genesis, 'In the beginning was the Word' (John 1.1). Nor is it an accident that the Gospels record the resurrection of Jesus happening in a garden – think the Garden of Eden. Creation stories are told all through the Bible, and return especially in Act 6 when there is a new creation. We will return to creation in Chapter 5; for now we move on to Act 2.

Act 2: The fall

What happens?

In this Act the good creation is messed up. This is how the world becomes the world as we know it, with death and violence, injustice and exploitation and all the other horrors it has to offer. The Bible pins this all on the way human beings, the crown of all creation, refuse their place in the created order. Human beings want to be gods, want to lord it over their fellow creatures. This, of course, is not possible, but the attempt destroys the good creation. Human beings end up unable to tell good from bad and worshipping that which is not God. More prosaically, Francis Spufford describes this as the 'human propensity to fuck things up' or the HPtFtU.[4] This captures what is going on in this act rather well.

Where is it found?

The real tragedy of the story of the Bible is that the fall happens almost immediately after creation – there is hardly any space between Acts 1 and 2. The story of the fall begins in Genesis 3 with the story of Adam and Eve eating the fruit they were told not to eat. It is followed by the story of the next generation, in which the first murder takes place – Cain kills his brother Abel (Genesis 4.1–16). After this, murder seems to become commonplace among the descendants of Adam, so that 'the earth is filled with violence' (Genesis 6.13). From here the book of Genesis tells the story of the tower of Babel (Genesis 11.1–9), in which the designs of human pride are thwarted by God. After this human beings are scattered throughout the world and are unable to understand one another easily.

What we have in Genesis 3—11 are stories that get gradually worse: the disobedience of Adam and Eve in eating the fruit; then the murder of Abel by Cain; then the widespread violence; then the human pride that is scattered and confused by God. At the root of all of this, according to the stories, is the desire to be more than human. The serpent tempts Eve by telling her that 'when you eat of it [the forbidden fruit] . . . you will be like God' (Genesis 3.5). Cain's murder of Abel is the opposite of the creator God. The tower of Babel is designed so that it has 'its top in the heavens' (Genesis 11.4). Genesis sees the origins of Spufford's HPtFtU in trying to reverse the creation of human beings. Instead of humans being made in the image of God, we humans try to make God in our own image. This is called 'idolatry', and the Bible as a whole can be read as a counterblast to idolatry in all its forms. The Psalms mock idolatry.

> Our God is in the heavens;
>   he does whatever he pleases.
> Their idols are silver and gold,
>   the work of human hands.
> They have mouths, but do not speak;
>   eyes, but do not see.
> They have ears, but do not hear;
>   noses, but do not smell.

> They have hands, but do not feel;
>> feet, but do not walk;
>> they make no sound in their throats.
> Those who make them are like them;
>> so are all who trust in them.
>
> (Psalm 115.3–8)

The last sentence is the devastating one. 'Those who make them are like them.' Idols are dead, and lead us to death.

What sort of stories?

It is worth pointing out that the stories in Acts 1 and 2 are not historical. We live in history with the consequences of both the good creation (Act 1) and the idolatrous HPtFtU (Act 2). The stories then are aetiological, told to explain why things are as they are. They help us to hold together the goodness of creation with the reality of our experience. The first two acts of this play are beyond the limits of human experience; they can only be spoken of indirectly.

Act 2a: Noah

What happens?

Before we move on into Act 3 it is worth spending some time on the story of Noah (Genesis 6—9). This story belongs to Act 2 – it is part of the Bible's telling of things going wrong and is told in the non-historical way that the first two acts have to be told. Yet it points ahead to how God will deal with that. In many ways it tells the story of the Bible in miniature.

What happens in the story is that God despairs. 'The LORD was sorry that he had made humankind on the earth, and it grieved him to his heart' (Genesis 6.6). So God decides to destroy human beings and start again. It's rather like a bad picture or piece of writing. We crumple it up and throw it into the waste-paper bin. But then God notices Noah, the only righteous person. Because of Noah, God saves Noah's whole family. But notice that the Bible never describes Noah's family as righteous. They appear to be like the rest of the human race, and are only saved because of their relationship to Noah. Through this one family God saves the whole world. Human beings and animals together. Noah and his family are given the chance to start again, to live in a new and recreated world. Finally God makes a covenant, a firm and unbreakable promise, with all creation that he will never try to drown the whole world again.

Links to other acts

The story of Noah speaks strongly of both the goodness of the creation (Act 1) and God's despair at the mess human beings make of it (Act 2). But we also see God acting to restore the creation through one family, just as we shall see God working through one family in Act 3. This focuses on one person, just as Act 4 shows the focusing of God's work on one person, that of Jesus. We also have hints of Act 6 in the new creation that Noah and his family are given. The theme of the making of a covenant will also be repeated – with Abraham, with Moses, in the promises of the prophets and in Jesus. The story of Noah is much more than a story about animals in pairs going on to a boat. It is the whole Bible in miniature!

Act 3: Israel

What happens?

Act 3 is the beginning of God's work to put right what went wrong in Act 2, without destroying everything and starting again (as we saw in Act 2a). God calls Abram, whose name is later changed to Abraham, so that in him 'all the families of the earth shall be blessed' (Genesis 12.3). Through Abraham, God calls a people – the people of Israel. The Bible records their struggles to be faithful – and at times downright refusal to be faithful – to the God who calls them. The plans of God become bound up in the life of a people.

Where do we find this?

Here we have the whole sweep of the Old Testament, from Genesis 12 to Malachi. It is helpful to think of this act in terms of a number of scenes.

Scene 1: Abraham and his family (Genesis 12—50)

Abraham is called, and from him the family of God's people is formed. Abraham is promised the land but does not himself possess it. There are twists and turns as the younger of Abraham's grandchildren (Jacob, whose name is later changed to Israel) is chosen as the one through whom the people of God will continue. Jacob's son Joseph is sold into slavery by his brothers but that turns out to have been providential in enabling the family to survive a famine by moving to Egypt.

Scene 2: The Exodus (Exodus—Deuteronomy)

This is possibly the defining scene. It opens with God's people numerous but enslaved in Egypt. Moses leads them into freedom and towards the Promised Land but despite the miraculous way they are freed, the people doubt God. At the point at which God gives them a covenant and a law by which to live, they make an idol to worship (Exodus 32), thus showing that the power of Act 2 remains intact.

Scene 3: The conquest of the Promised Land (Joshua, Judges and Ruth)

Under the leadership of Joshua the people of Israel conquer the Promised Land. The difficulties of living together as God's people in the land begin to show. After Joshua's death Israel is ruled by a series of judges – charismatic leaders who keep Israel faithful to God and secure from her enemies. In this scene Israel's enemies are mostly the Philistines, and throughout it things deteriorate. There is a repeated cycle of Israel being threatened by the Philistines; a judge being called by God to defend Israel; Israel living in peace for a time. But the end of each cycle is never as good as the beginning and the scene spirals downwards. By the end of this scene Israel is in a poor state, unable to hear the guidance of God. As the next scene opens we read that 'the word of the LORD was rare in those days' (1 Samuel 3.1).

Scene 4: The kings of Israel (1 Samuel—2 Chronicles; Psalms; wisdom literature)

This scene opens with the call of Samuel, the greatest of Israel's judges. He restores the people to God and gives them security. But the people want a king. Despite Samuel's warnings and his fear that this is replacing God's role as the king of Israel, God grants the people their request. The first king, Saul, is disobedient. His fall allows the great king David, whom God describes as 'a man after his own heart' (1 Samuel 13.14), to come to the throne. David too is flawed. He commits adultery and murders the husband of the woman he desires. But he is also the great writer of Psalms.

David's son Solomon, the pinnacle of Israel's monarchy, builds the Temple, the place where God dwells on earth. Solomon is renowned for his wisdom, a gift from God. But Solomon also brings false gods into Israel. Under his son Rehoboam the kingdom splits into Israel in the north and Judah in the south. Few kings of either kingdom are faithful to God and ultimately the northern kingdom falls to the Assyrian empire. It is never heard of again. Judah continues for a while longer before it too falls to Babylon.

Scene 5: The exile (Jeremiah, Lamentations, Ezekiel, Isaiah 40—55)

In 603 BC the armies of Babylon besieged Jerusalem and demanded tribute from King Jehoiakim of Judah. He paid. But six years later they came back for more. Jehoiakim either could not or would not pay more tribute and Jerusalem fell to Nebuchadnezzar, king of Babylon, in 597 BC. The city was devastated, the king killed and the Temple looted. A first group of exiles, largely from the royal family and the ruling elite, were taken back to Babylon. Ten years later the king in Jerusalem, King Zedekiah, rose up against Babylon. Again Jerusalem was besieged and this time the city and the Temple were destroyed. In Babylon the prophet Ezekiel saw a vision of the Temple become so corrupt that God withdrew his presence from it before the Babylonian army destroyed it (Ezekiel 11).

The exile should have been the end of the people of Judah. They should have gone to Babylon and become part of the cosmopolitan mix of the imperial city. The gods of Babylon had defeated the God of Israel, as the armies of Babylon overran those of Judah. But that is not how the Bible records it. Rather than God being defeated, the exiled people of Israel saw that God had allowed their defeat as a punishment for their faithlessness to God's covenant. The prophets had predicted that this would happen and had also promised restoration once God's anger had subsided. That gave them hope for the future, and they held on to their faith in God while they were in exile. This also enabled them to hold on to their identity as a people. The exile is an amazingly formative time for the people of Israel and for the Bible. Its significance cannot really be overestimated.

Scene 6: The Restoration (Ezra, Nehemiah, later prophets)

When Cyrus, king of Persia, captured Babylon in 539 BC the exiles were finally allowed to return home. The following year Cyrus issued a decree allowing the Israelites to return home and to rebuild the city of Jerusalem and the Temple (Ezra 1.2–4). Through great struggles the Temple was rededicated. But the great promises of the prophets – Isaiah, Jeremiah and Ezekiel – were not fulfilled by this. Israel was still oppressed by those around her; her people were still a mixture of faithful and faithless; there was no great vision of God returning to the Temple to reverse that seen by Ezekiel. Some began to question whether this restoration was complete. Hopes for a future act of God remained strong.

The writing of the Old Testament

The Old Testament is the product of Act 3. It contains features that point back to Acts 1 and 2, which remain outside experience. Similarly it contains passages that point forward to Act 6, also outside the realms of experience. But the Bible is not written at the height of monarchy, with Israel at the pinnacle of its existence. Instead it is mostly written in exile, and what was written earlier was edited and brought into its final form at this time. In exile the Torah (Law) is given its final and authoritative form; the histories are written up so that they point to the faithlessness of the people and the resulting exile; the writings of the prophets are gathered together so that the judgement of God can be heard. As I have suggested already, the Bible is not written from a great vantage point from which all of history can be surveyed. Rather, it is written in the middle of things, in exile, in a time and a place of powerlessness and oppression.

Act 4: Jesus

What happens?

Jesus, baptized by John the Baptist in the river Jordan, spends his ministry in Galilee and Jerusalem. He teaches about the kingdom of God, heals, casts out demons and gathers a group of disciples. He is hailed as Messiah, the promised leader who will bring in the time in which all God's promises will be fulfilled. But a conspiracy of the religious leaders and the Roman occupiers of Jerusalem execute him. He appears to have failed. And then three days later he is seen again by his disciples, risen from the dead. He gathers them together once more, promises them the Holy Spirit and then leaves them to return to God.

Where is it found?

Jesus' story is told in the four Gospels – Matthew, Mark, Luke and John – and in the first chapter of the Acts of the Apostles. A few quotations from Jesus are included in passages of Paul's letters.

How does this relate to Acts 1 to 3?

All of the Gospels relate Jesus to creation (Act 1), and Matthew and John both begin their Gospel with direct allusions to Genesis 1. Jesus' resurrection is spoken of in terms of new creation, which has allusions to both Act 1 and Act 6. Above all, however, Jesus is presented as following the pattern of the life of Israel (Act 3). From baptism in the Jordan, which the people of Israel crossed to enter the Promised Land, to spending 40 days in the wilderness being tempted; from going up a mountain to meet with Moses, Elijah and God, to quoting the Psalms as he hangs on the cross, Jesus is presented as mirroring the life of the people of Israel, while remaining faithful to God.

Act 5: The Church

What happens?

From small and unpromising beginnings the followers of Jesus are given the gift of the Holy Spirit. They form a growing community in Jerusalem. As persecution forces them out they form new communities in the neighbouring cities. Missionaries plant Christian communities or churches throughout the Mediterranean world, even in Rome itself. This includes both Jews and Gentiles, who come together in following Jesus. Most notable among these missionaries is Paul, a Jew and a Pharisee who initially tried to arrest and kill Christians. This is a time of great expansion, and much improvisation in the light of what Jesus said and did. Paul's letters in particular show the development of a theology exploring and explaining the effect of Jesus on thinking about God. It is also a time of great argument. For the earliest Church, the argument was about whether one had to become a Jew first before becoming a Christian. This meant following the rules about food and, for men, being circumcised. Paul's letters are full of real anger about those who would require those becoming Christians to be circumcised. On one occasion he says that he wishes they would go the whole hog and 'castrate themselves' (Galatians 5.12). Argument has been present in the Church since the earliest days.

Where is it found?

The story of the Church can be found in the Acts of the Apostles and in the letters of the New Testament. The largest part of these are written by Paul (or claiming to be by Paul), but there are also letters by (or claiming to be by) Peter, James, John, Jude and an anonymous letter to Hebrew Christians.

The unfinished act

This act of the story of the Bible has not finished, it continues. There is no clear ending, no moment at which the New Testament finishes. Instead the New Testament seems to record the events of the first generation after Jesus. After that we are into the improvisation that starts with the first five acts and leads to Act 6.

It is also worth noting that, just as in Act 3, the Bible is written in a place of incompleteness and weakness. The Gospels seem to have been written down as the first Apostles were dying, so that a record of Jesus' acts could be retained. The letters are occasional pieces, often dealing with specific problems in specific communities.

The Church in the time that the New Testament is written is weak and often persecuted. It is not a strong community, able to impose its will.

Act 6: *The new creation*

What happens?

In the final act of the play, all God's promises are brought to fulfilment. The consequences of tragedy in Act 2 are overcome, the faithful people of God are brought back to life to enjoy heaven come to join with earth. This act is only glimpsed 'in a mirror, dimly' (1 Corinthians 13.12), but the visions the Bible offers are quite wonderful. The book of Revelation offers this vision:

> See, the home of God is among mortals. He will dwell with them; they will be his peoples, and God himself will be with them; he will wipe every tear from their eyes. Death will be no more; mourning and crying and pain will be no more, for the first things have passed away.   (Revelation 21.3–4)

Where do we find this?

These visions and promises are found all over the Bible. The prophets, especially, offer important contributions to this vision (Isaiah 11 and 65 are two of the greatest examples). Jesus also offers this vision (see, for example, Matthew 25). Even Paul's letters contain material that contributes to the vision (Romans 8 is the best example). Above all the books of Daniel and Revelation contain visions of the new creation that inspire and offer hope.

Where do we see this from?

These visions of the new creation remain exactly that – visions. They are glimpses, pictures, ideas, promises seen from within Acts 3 and 5. For Christians they are focused by the story of Jesus in Act 4, and especially his resurrection. Act 6, offered to us in glimpses, is outside experience, just like Act 1. It remains a mystery.

This model of a six-act play fits the Bible well. It enables us to understand the grand sweep of the Bible and to place individual passages within it. More than that, however, it enables us to see our place as in the middle of the story. The story is not over.

Try it out

1 Read a children's Bible and get to know the stories of the Bible.
2 Watch an episode of a television programme. What would you have happen next in the story?

Further reading

Brian D. McLaren, *The Story We Find Ourselves In: Further Adventures of a New Kind of Christian*, Chichester: Wiley, 2003; repr. London: SPCK, 2013.

Samuel Wells, *Improvisation: The Drama of Christian Ethics*, London: SPCK, 2004.

4

The stories of Jesus

——————•◦•——————

The Bible is the cradle wherein Christ is laid.
Martin Luther[1]

A story of Jesus

Let's begin with a story.

> Someone gave a great dinner and invited many. At the time
> for the dinner he sent his slave to say to those who had been
> invited, 'Come; for everything is ready now.' But they all alike
> began to make excuses. The first said to him, 'I have bought a
> piece of land, and I must go out and see it; please accept my
> apologies.' Another said, 'I have bought five yoke of oxen, and
> I am going to try them out; please accept my apologies.' Another
> said, 'I have just been married, and therefore I cannot come.'
> So the slave returned and reported this to his master. Then the
> owner of the house became angry and said to his slave, 'Go out
> at once into the streets and lanes of the town and bring in the
> poor, the crippled, the blind, and the lame.' And the slave said,
> 'Sir, what you ordered has been done, and there is still room.'
> Then the master said to the slave, 'Go out into the roads and
> lanes, and compel people to come in, so that my house may be
> filled. For I tell you, none of those who were invited will taste
> my dinner.'   (Luke 14.16–24)

Dinner parties are an important image in the Bible. They are used
as images of the coming kingdom of God. So Isaiah writes that 'the
Lord of hosts will make for all peoples a feast of rich food, a feast
of well-matured wines' (Isaiah 25.6). This story tells us something
about the kingdom of God. It is told to explain some advice Jesus

gives to a host at a meal to which he has been invited. He says to his host:

> When you give a luncheon or a dinner, do not invite your friends or your brothers or your relatives or rich neighbours, in case they may invite you in return, and you would be repaid. But when you give a banquet, invite the poor, the crippled, the lame, and the blind. And you will be blessed, because they cannot repay you, for you will be repaid at the resurrection of the righteous.   (Luke 14.12–14)

So this is a story told to explain how someone should live to prepare for the kingdom of God. It also appears a bit rude, the guest telling the host how he should organize his parties. Perhaps that is why Jesus tells this in the form of a story – it softens it a bit, and means that the host is left with something to think about. Certainly this is a story that contains division, and the guests originally invited do not come out of it well. It is also a story that invites us into its world and may not let us out without changing us!

Stories like this one are the characteristic form of Jesus' teaching. They are called 'parables'. The Bible tells several parables, beginning in the Old Testament. The prophet Nathan is sent to King David to tell him that he has committed a crime in committing adultery with Bathsheba and then having her husband killed. He approaches this task carefully, and tells a story about a rich man stealing a little ewe lamb from a poor man. David is incensed by the story and says that 'the man who has done this deserves to die.' At this point Nathan tells him, 'You are the man!' (2 Samuel 12.1–7). Here we see a parable used to approach the truth carefully and in a way that allows the teller to say something potentially dangerous. Nathan invites David into the story, and so to pronounce judgement on himself.

Jesus tells most of the parables in the Bible. His parables are stories about the kingdom of God and about the people of God. He uses images that are familiar to his hearers and drawn from elsewhere in the Bible. But the stories lead to unexpected outcomes. So in the story that begins this chapter, the people who are invited to the feast refuse the invitation. In their place all kinds of people, but especially the poor and the outcast, are brought into the party. This is Jesus telling a story about God and his kingdom, using images from the Bible. He introduces an unexpected twist (the refusal of the invitation), which changes the expected conclusion. It is also a story that helps to explain what Jesus himself is doing. He spends his time not with the religious leaders or the great and the good but among the poor and the ill, the unclean and the morally dubious. If he were to stand up and teach this directly he would be telling the whole establishment that their understanding of God and his promises was wrong. He probably wouldn't last long. So he tells a story instead and invites them to draw their own conclusions about their place in that story.

Parables are, therefore, stories that obscure as well as illuminate. They are safe ways of telling difficult and uncomfortable truths. When Jesus does simply tell things without using parables, it gets difficult. In his hometown of Nazareth, Jesus reads from the prophet Isaiah and is invited to preach. He tells his hearers that the prophecy he has read has been fulfilled, and they are amazed. But when he goes on to tell them that this means that the Gentiles will also be welcome in God's kingdom, they are enraged and try to kill him (Luke 4.16–30). Perhaps that is why he used parables so much!

The story of Jesus

Jesus as Israel

The story of Jesus, as we saw in Chapter 3, is a retelling of the story of Israel. In explaining this, let us start with his baptism by John in the river Jordan. That is the point that all four Gospels agree was the beginning of his narrative. Immediately we are faced with a challenge. John baptized people as they confessed their sins. Yet Christians have seen Jesus as 'tested as we are, yet without sin' (Hebrews 4.15). Why then was he baptized? The Gospel writers themselves saw this problem. Matthew has John try to stop Jesus; Luke quietly slips in Jesus' baptism (still by John) after he has told the story of John being arrested; John never quite mentions that Jesus was baptized. In being baptized, Jesus identifies himself with the people of God. They came through the Red Sea, and then the Jordan, to enter into the

Promised Land. This is reinforced by the way the voice from heaven describes Jesus as God's 'beloved son' (Matthew 3.17; Mark 1.11; Luke 3.22), which is the way God describes the people of Israel to Pharaoh (Exodus 4.22–23). Matthew, Mark and Luke all continue the story by having Jesus sent into the wilderness for 40 days. Again, the echoes of the people of Israel journeying through the wilderness to the Promised Land are clear.

While in the wilderness Jesus, like the people of Israel, is tempted. The temptations also are retelling the story of Israel. Almost as soon as the people of Israel were free from Egypt they began to complain that they did not have enough to eat (Exodus 16.2–3). And so Jesus' first temptation is to turn stones into bread. When they came to the next place in the wilderness, which Moses calls Massah and Meribah, the people of Israel complained that there was nothing to drink (Exodus 17.1–7). The people of Israel put God to the test by asking 'Is the LORD among us or not?' (Exodus 17.7). In his second temptation Jesus rebukes the Devil, quoting from a passage that in full reads 'Do not put the LORD your God to the test, as you tested him at Massah' (Deuteronomy 6.16). Finally the third temptation, for which the Devil takes Jesus up a very high mountain, recalls Mount Sinai on which Moses receives the Law. Famously, while Moses was in the presence of God receiving the Law, the people of Israel were forging an idol – the golden calf – and worshipping it (Exodus 32). The temptation stories tell the story of Jesus in terms of the story of the people of Israel in the wilderness, and show Jesus being faithful to his calling.

Throughout his ministry Jesus speaks of the kingdom of God. In the prayer he taught his followers he taught them to pray for its coming. The kingdom of God is, if nothing else, Israel. Israel was the kingdom in which God was king rather than a human ruler. When this changed, the kings were seen as anointed by God. In speaking of the kingdom of God, Jesus is speaking of the fulfilment of God's promises to the people of Israel. Israel is to be restored as a nation; Israel is to be a place other nations look to for help and as a paradigm of how to be a nation; Israel is to be the place where God wins a great victory over all that is wrong. In talking about the kingdom of God, Jesus evoked all of these promises. He reminded people of the incompleteness of the restoration after the exile. Jesus embodies Israel, he is a faithful Israel. He also comes to bring to fulfilment all of God's promises for the people of Israel. That is what we turn to now.

Jesus as Messiah

There are other ways the story of Jesus is written as the story of Israel. He calls 12 disciples as leaders in his new movement, and this is a clear reminder of the 12 tribes of Israel. It also seems to be a way of placing himself as the leader of the people of Israel, as the king. This is how Jesus fulfilled the promises for the Messiah. 'Messiah' simply means 'anointed one' (the Greek translation of this is 'Christ', which is not a surname for Jesus but a way of referring to him as the Messiah or king). It refers to the way kings were anointed in oil as a sign of God's blessing and calling to be the king.

Jesus seems to have been recognized as the Messiah during his lifetime but the Gospels show him nervous of using the title himself. When the crowds come to make him king he 'withdraws' (John 6.15), he hides away. Yet when he enters Jerusalem at the start of the last week of his life, Jesus is riding on a donkey (Matthew 21.1–11; Mark 11.1–11; Luke 19.29–40). This deliberately recalls the prophecy of Zechariah that 'your king comes to you; triumphant and victorious is he, humble and riding on a donkey' (Zechariah 9.9).

The reason Jesus is both cautious in using the title 'Messiah', and yet can act in ways that seem to claim the role, is that he is trying to offer an understanding of what it is to be the Messiah that is different from what is expected by his contemporaries. There was no simple list of things stating what it was to be the Messiah that could be ticked off, but there was a collection of ideas that came together to offer the material for recognizing the Messiah. Three in particular are worth noting.

- The Messiah would bring in the age of the fulfilment of God's promises.
- The Messiah would restore the Temple, just as the great kings David and Solomon had planned and built the Temple.
- The Messiah would fight Israel's battles and free the people from their oppressors.

It is easy to see Jesus fulfilling the first two of these ideas. His teaching about the kingdom of God did indeed claim to be fulfilling God's promises. His clearing of the Temple could be a sign of his restoring it to its proper functions. But Jesus was no military leader, and could even be compassionate to the forces occupying Israel at the time.

It is the closeness of Jesus to these expectations of the Messiah that explains why he was killed – and thus why he was cautious of using the title. When Pilate orders the charge against him to read 'The King of the Jews' (Matthew 27.37; Mark 15.26; Luke 23.38; John 19.19–22), he is both mocking Jesus and pointedly reminding the people of who is really in charge. Had Jesus been the Messiah, surely he would have been overseeing a military offensive to free Israel from the Romans rather than dying. No one had ever heard of a crucified Messiah.

And yet the Gospels, and Christians ever since, have wanted to say that Jesus really was the Messiah. Pilate was strangely right in the charge that he placed above Jesus' head as he died on the cross. Jesus had set his sights on enemies of Israel, indeed enemies of the whole of creation, which were far more afflicting than an invading army or a corrupt leadership, although they could be seen within these things. These enemies were sin and death. In terms of our six-act play introduced in the last chapter, it is as if Jesus' contemporaries were seeing the enemies the Messiah would defeat as those within Act 3, so that the Romans become the equivalent of the Philistines. Jesus, however, sees the real enemies as those causing and caused by Act 2. Thus he is the fulfilment of the role of Abraham and the people called in his name to defeat these enemies and rescue all creation from them. When Jesus dies on the cross, John's Gospel records that he says 'It is finished' (John 19.30). This is not a cry of defeat but a victory cry that says he has accomplished everything he came to do. The Messiah has won his victory. The resurrection of Jesus is not a reversal of the defeat of his death, rather it is a vindication of Jesus' understanding of the vocation of the Messiah and a sign of the victory won in his death. It is the first fruits of the restored and renewed creation (Act 6).

This is a much bigger vision than that of a nationalist Messiah. It reshapes everything around it, including how we read the Bible. Luke's Gospel tells a story of two of Jesus' disciples walking away from Jerusalem on the day of the resurrection. They are in despair and a stranger walks with them, asking them what has gone wrong. They had hoped Jesus would restore Israel, they tell him, but he was crucified. As far as they are concerned, that is the end of the story. The stranger tells them they have not understood the Bible, and patiently explains how it tells that the Messiah has to suffer and die and then enter into glory. Finally the two disciples recognize the stranger as Jesus. This story (Luke 24.13–35) is one of the greatest of the resurrection stories and shows how the death and resurrection of Jesus change the way the Messiah and the whole Bible are to be understood.

Jesus as God

The Bible also describes Jesus in terms that can only really mean that he is God as well. John's Gospel is the most blunt when it says: 'In the beginning was the Word, and the Word was with God, and the Word was God' (John 1.1). Paul's letters also speak in this way on occasion, so he writes to the Philippians that 'Christ Jesus . . . was in the form of God, [but] did not regard equality with God as something to be exploited' (Philippians 2.5–6).

The other Gospels also speak of Jesus in ways that can only really mean they think Jesus is God. Matthew speaks of Jesus fulfilling Isaiah's prophecy of Emmanuel, which means 'God is with us' (Matthew 1.23). All the Gospels record Jesus purporting to forgive people's sins, and the charges of blasphemy that follow this (Matthew 9.1–8; Mark 2.1–12; Luke 5.17–26; 7.48–49; John 9). Mark records that Jesus calms a storm, which results in his disciples being afraid and asking 'Who then is this, that even the wind and the sea obey him?' (Mark 4.41). The implication is that Jesus is taking the role God has in being the master of the chaotic power of the sea. On another occasion Mark records that Jesus is walking on water towards the boat in which are his disciples. Mark says that 'He intended to pass them by' (Mark 6.48). This is another description of Jesus in terms of God. God tells Moses that Moses cannot see his face and live, but that he will *pass by* Moses so that he can see his face (Exodus 33.21–23). There are numerous occasions, in the Gospels and in the rest of the New Testament, when people worship Jesus. This too is evidence for his being thought of in terms of God.

This is not an exhaustive list but it is an indication that the Bible, in direct and indirect ways, paints a picture of Jesus that includes his identification with God. The New Testament does not present an account of this that has all of its theological and philosophical implications worked out – it took the Christian Church about 300 years to do that, and there is a case for suggesting that theologians are still working on it. But the raw material is there in the New Testament, and especially in the Gospels.

The stories of Jesus – the Gospels

The Gospels are stories of Jesus. They collect those stories told when the early Christians gathered for worship, itself perhaps a sign that they were valued as much as the Old Testament. The Gospels date from the end of the first generation of Christians. Perhaps most importantly, they date from the time when the apostles, those who had followed Jesus in his lifetime (Acts 1.21–22), were dying out, either from old age or from persecution. Two of the four Gospels in the New Testament (Matthew and John) are attributed to members of Jesus' chosen 12 disciples. Mark is closely associated in Christian tradition with Peter, and Luke with Paul.

Mark's Gospel is usually thought to have been the earliest Gospel to have been written, and dates for this vary from around AD 68 to 72. What that means is that Mark is written around the time of the Jewish rebellion against Rome, which began in 66 and ended in 70 when the Romans levelled Jerusalem and destroyed the Temple. All the Gospels were probably completed by the end of the first century and almost certainly by 110. (Scholars, being scholars, continue to argue with pretty much all of this!) The earliest fragment of the Gospels we have is part of John 18, which was found in an Egyptian market by Bernard Grenfell in 1920. It dates to about 135, by which time John's Gospel must have been copied and a copy sent to Egypt. A very few people think that we have an even earlier fragment of Mark's Gospel (from chapter 6) among the scrolls recovered at Qumran beside the Dead Sea. It is known as 7Q5 (because it was found in the seventh cave at Qumran). These scrolls were abandoned in about AD 68 as the Romans retook the country. If this is so then

Mark, at least, was written much earlier than most think. However, this is a very small fragment – only 20 characters – and there are many other ways of interpreting it. Most scholars think it very unlikely that this is part of Mark's Gospel.

As the Church moved into a generation without the leadership of those who had travelled in Galilee with Jesus, it needed to record their stories so that they could continue to be told. These stories would have been told over and over again, so that they are shaped by the telling as well as by the stories they record. In writing them down, the Gospel writers shaped them again as parts of the story of Jesus they were telling. This triple shaping of the stories – by the events in the life of Jesus; by the Church passing them down; by the Gospel writers writing them down – means that we always hear of Jesus through others.

The Gospels are not dispassionate biographies of Jesus. John spells out his aim that 'these are written so that you may come to believe that Jesus is the Messiah, the Son of God, and that through believing you may have life in his name' (John 20.31). Luke writes that he has tried 'to write an orderly account . . . so that you may know the truth concerning the things about which you have been instructed' (Luke 1.3–4). Matthew and Mark have no equivalent statements but it is hard to think that they would have disagreed with either John's concern to help readers believe or Luke's to set out the truth. These are books designed to involve readers and help them follow the Jesus they meet in their pages.

The Synoptic problem

The first three Gospels are very similar, even down to using exactly the same words. These Gospels are sometimes called the 'Synoptic Gospels' after the practice of setting out passages in parallel columns so that the similarities and differences can be seen. Those passages found in all three Synoptic Gospels are called the 'triple tradition'. This offers us an important window into how the Gospels were written. Trying to decipher why Matthew, Mark and Luke are so similar and what that tells us about how the Gospels were written is sometimes called the 'Synoptic problem'. One helpful example to explore this problem is illustrated by the comparison of three passages overleaf.

Matthew 16.24–28	Mark 8.34—9.1	Luke 9.23–27
[24]Then Jesus told *his disciples*, '*If any want to become my followers, let them deny themselves and take up their cross and follow me.* [25]*For those who want to save their life will lose it, and those who lose their life for my sake will* find *it.*	[34]**He** called the crowd with *his disciples,* and **said to them**, '*If any* **want to become my followers, let them deny themselves and take up their cross and follow me.** [35]**For those who want to save their life will lose it, and those who lose their life for my sake**, and for the sake of the gospel, **will save** it.	[23]Then **he said to them** all, '*If any want to become my followers, let them deny themselves and take up their cross* daily *and follow me.* [24]*For those who want to save their life will lose it,* and those who lose their *life for my sake will* save *it.*
[26]*For what* will *it profit them* if they *gain the whole world but forfeit their life?* Or *what* will they give in return for their life?	[36]**For what** will **it profit them** to **gain the whole world** and **forfeit** their life? [37]Indeed, **what** can they give in return for their life? **Those who are ashamed of me and of my words** in this adulterous and sinful generation, **of them the**	[25]*What* does *it profit them* if they *gain the whole world, but* lose or *forfeit* themselves? [26]**Those who are ashamed of me and of my words,**
[27]'*For the Son of Man* is to *come* with his *angels in the glory of his Father,* and then he will repay everyone for what has been done.	**Son of Man will** also **be ashamed when he comes in the glory of his Father with the holy angels.'**	of them *the Son of Man* **will be ashamed when he** *comes* in his **glory** and *the glory of* the *Father* and **of the holy** *angels*.
[28]*Truly I tell you, there are some standing here who will not taste death* before *they see the* Son of Man *coming* in his *kingdom.*'	[9.1]And he said to them, '**Truly I tell you, there are some standing here who will not taste death** until **they see** that **the kingdom** of God has **come** with power.	[27]But *truly I tell you, there are some standing here who will not taste death* before *they see the* **kingdom** of God.

I have underlined agreements between Matthew and Mark, set out in **bold print** agreements between **Mark and Luke** and used *italics* for agreements between *Matthew and Luke*.

What this enables us to see is how in this piece of the triple tradition, the order of the passage, and even the words, show that Mark is the common feature from which the others deviate – as and when they do. There is very little of the passage – only four English words – in which Matthew and Luke agree against Mark. For the far greater part, both in volume and in substance, Mark is the middle term from which Matthew and Luke move away and to which they also return. About 90 per cent of Mark's Gospel is found in Matthew and more than half in Luke. Mark provides the order in which the events happen, and if one of Matthew or Luke doesn't follow Mark's order then the other does. There are no occasions when Matthew's and Luke's order of events agrees against Mark.

There are, in addition, about 200 verses that are common to Matthew and Luke but not found in Mark. They are almost all sayings, and the verbatim agreement varies from almost entirely verbatim accounts to virtually no verbal agreement while telling the same story. Nor are they arranged in the same order in the two Gospels. If Mark is the middle term of the three Gospels, there is also some significant agreement of Matthew and Luke beyond Mark.

These two observations have given rise to the normal answer given to the Synoptic problem: Mark was written first, Matthew and Luke used Mark – and copied much of it – in writing their Gospels. They also used a second source (often called 'Q', from the German *Quelle*, meaning 'source'), which we no longer have. This does not solve everything: there are still minor agreements between Matthew and Luke against Mark, for example. But it is the best overall solution.

Other Gospels?

If there ever was a document like Q, used by both Matthew and Luke, it is, as I have said, now lost. There are other parts of the Gospel stories that also seem to demonstrate that there were more stories of Jesus than we have in the Gospels. The famous story of the woman caught in adultery (John 8.53—9.11) seems not to fit where it is placed in most Bibles – mine has it as a long footnote. This interrupts a continuous passage in John's Gospel, and the Gospel makes better sense if it is taken out. The earliest manuscripts omit the story. There is a great deal of variation in where early manuscripts of the Gospels place this story. Some make it part of Luke's Gospel (placing it after Luke 21.38) or elsewhere in John's Gospel (either after John 7.36 or after John 21.25 as an appendix to the Gospel). In fact the story belongs in none of these places but was a story of Jesus deemed too good to lose. It was rammed in where it didn't fit so that it wasn't lost.

There are also whole gospels that are not included in the Bible. In 2006, to great publicity, the Gospel of Judas was 'discovered' – in fact it was already well known – and created a media storm. It consists of supposed conversations between Jesus and Judas. These were secret conversations, away from the other disciples and followers. In this regard it can stand for a number of gospels that originate in the late second century and are part of a movement within and beyond Christianity called 'Gnosticism'. This movement highlighted secret knowledge (in Greek, *gnosis*), and so a book of secret conversations between Jesus and a disciple was a perfect way of teaching the Gnostic way. These 'Gnostic Gospels' are interesting for those concerned with the history of religious innovation; but they tell us very little about Jesus.

One possible exception to this is the Gospel of Thomas. Thomas is a short book, comprising a collection of 116 sayings and no narrative stories. This makes it alike to the – hypothetical – document Q. Significantly, Thomas has no account of the death and resurrection of Jesus, although one story makes an allusion to it. Thomas in its current form belongs with the Gnostic Gospels of the second century. However, there does seem to be some evidence that it contains sayings of Jesus that go back very early, possibly even to Jesus himself. Weeding these out from the more Gnostic background is hard, and creates many scholarly arguments. But Thomas might be an additional source of material from Jesus. It was not considered for inclusion in the New Testament but may offer us exciting glimpses of extra material about Jesus.

The four Gospels in the New Testament are different from one another. Mark is abrupt, mysterious and always moving on. Matthew is concerned with Jesus as a good Jew, fulfilling the law – he collects Jesus' teaching into five blocks, reflecting the five books of the Torah. Luke is well ordered and concerned for the outsider, perhaps because he is a Gentile – his Gospel has a second volume, the Acts of the Apostles, which describes what happens as the early Church spreads the good news about Jesus. John is meditative and reflective, always looking for the deeper meaning of a story. But all four Gospels live in the same world. All are concerned to help the reader follow Jesus and enter into his stories.

Try it out

1 Read the parable of the two sons (Luke 15.11–32) and imagine yourself into the story. What questions are left unanswered? How would you answer them?

2 Read Mark 8.27–33 and consider how you might answer Jesus' question.

Further reading

John W. Drane, *Jesus and the Four Gospels*, Tring: Lion, 1979.

Richard A. Burridge, *Four Gospels, One Jesus? A Symbolic Reading*, London: SPCK, 1994; 2nd edn 2005; reissued 2013.

5

Praying with the Bible

———◆•◆•◆———

Reading the Bible without meditating on it is like trying
to eat without swallowing.

Anon.

The first of my ten 'commandments' for Bible reading may be to pray,
but there is more to say about prayer and the Bible. In this chapter
we will explore prayers in the Bible, prayers taken from the Bible and
a method of praying with the Bible.

Prayers in the Bible

It should not come as much of a surprise that the Bible contains
prayers. The very beginning of the Bible looks a lot like an act of
worship, with God's repeated refrain that 'it was good' (Genesis 1.12,
18, 25, 31). The Bible ends with not one but two prayers: 'Amen.
Come, Lord Jesus! The grace of the Lord Jesus be with all the saints.
Amen' (Revelation 22.20–21). In between there are many prayers.
There are instructions for the Temple in which prayers are to be said.
There is an instruction to 'pray without ceasing' (1 Thessalonians
5.17). Prayer is an important theme within the Bible.

Some of the basic Christian prayers come from the Bible. One
favourite is the Grace:

> The grace of our Lord Jesus Christ,
> the love of God,
> and the fellowship of the Holy Spirit
> be with us all, ever more. Amen.

This comes from the end of Paul's second letter to the Corinthians
(2 Corinthians 13.13). It is a simple prayer of blessing, distinguished

by the way it invokes God, Jesus and the Holy Spirit separately. Standing at the end of Paul's most personal and painful letter, it speaks of grace, love and fellowship – themes throughout Paul's letter. When Christians pray this prayer they are asking that they might know the free gift of Jesus, the love of God that spared nothing to reach his fallen world, and a life lived together with God and with one another. It is a simple prayer. Living it out is a life's work and more.

The Lord's Prayer

Two of the Gospels, Matthew and Luke, give versions of the Lord's Prayer. They are subtly different, and different as well from the normal version of the prayer said by Christians. I have set them out below.

Matthew 6.9–13	Luke 11.2–4	The Lord's Prayer
Our Father in heaven, hallowed be your name. Your kingdom come. Your will be done, on earth as it is in heaven.	Father, hallowed be your name. Your kingdom come.	Our Father in heaven, hallowed be your name, your kingdom come, your will be done, on earth as in heaven.
Give us this day our daily bread.	Give us each day our daily bread.	Give us today our daily bread.
And forgive us our debts, as we also have forgiven our debtors.	And forgive us our sins, for we ourselves forgive everyone indebted to us.	Forgive us our sins as we forgive those who sin against us.
And do not bring us to the time of trial, but rescue us from the evil one.	And do not bring us to the time of trial.	Lead us not into temptation but deliver us from evil.
		For the kingdom, the power, and the glory are yours now and for ever.

They are recognizably the same prayer, despite their differences. The ending of the prayer as many Christians pray it is not in the Gospel versions (although some manuscripts do include it, a sign that the ending dates from very early in the life of the Church), and the Roman Catholic tradition doesn't use it. But all it does is return to the sense of the kingdom and the holiness of God, with which the prayer begins. It is not a major addition to the meaning of the prayer.

The Lord's Prayer is inseparable from the life and teaching of Jesus. Its opening address to 'Our Father' reminds us of Jesus' distinctive and intimate address to God. At his baptism a voice from heaven declares that Jesus is 'my Son, the Beloved' (Matthew 3.17; Mark 1.11; Luke 3.22). In teaching his disciples to pray like this, Jesus invites us into this relationship of love with God.

When the prayer prays 'Your kingdom come' it taps into the heart of Jesus' teaching. The whole of the Lord's Prayer refers to the kingdom of God – it is a kingdom prayer. Praying for the kingdom of God to come is praying for God's promises to be fulfilled and for peace and justice to be seen throughout the world. To pray this is also to commit oneself to a life in tune with the values of the kingdom of God. This is not an easy option. As the prayer continues with 'on earth as in heaven', the clear implication is that this is a fairly rare occurrence. To pray for the kingdom is to swim against the stream.

The prayer continues with a prayer for daily bread. This too is about the kingdom of God. It recalls the many meals Jesus had with his disciples and with all kinds of people. It recalls the times Jesus fed thousands of people with scant resources. It recalls his last meal, when he took bread, blessed it, broke it and gave it to his disciples as his body. All of these meals are signs of the kingdom. They recall the great banquets promised by Isaiah, when 'the LORD of hosts will make for all peoples a feast of rich food' (Isaiah 25.6). All of these meals are also occasions at which Jesus is criticized and the seeds of his rejection are sown. But this is also a prayer that God will meet our basic needs, our daily bread. Those of us who never have to worry about having enough to eat each day may never know the deepest meaning of the Lord's Prayer.

We now come to the prayer that God will 'forgive us our sins, as we forgive those who sin against us'. Here Matthew and Luke both speak of forgiving debts. This too is a kingdom reference. Luke begins his account of Jesus' ministry with Jesus claiming to fulfil Isaiah's prophecy of 'the year of the Lord's favour' (Luke 4.19, quoting Isaiah 61.2). This in turn speaks of the year of Jubilee, the fiftieth year when all debts would be forgiven (Leviticus 25). The coming of the kingdom of God will bring release from the slavery of debt. It is a prayer that continues to be relevant, even in rich countries. But it is also more than that, just as what enslaves us is more than that. Luke speaks of being forgiven our sins, the wrongdoing that also enslaves us. Forgiving others their debt is a sign of and a response to the forgiveness of our sins. In Matthew's Gospel, Jesus says that our forgiveness and God's are bound up together: 'if you forgive others their trespasses, your heavenly Father will also forgive you; but if you do not forgive others, neither will your Father forgive your trespasses' (Matthew 6.14–15).

Finally, in the biblical version of the Lord's Prayer we come to the request not to be led into temptation. Here the biblical original is very helpful in understanding the prayer. The Gospels have the prayer asking 'do not bring us to the time of trial.' This is not about asking for help resisting a third chocolate biscuit. It is asking God not to put us in a place where our faith and commitment will be tested so much that we might fail. Christians are not to seek out times of suffering for their faith; indeed we are to pray that we be spared them. Paul was confident that God 'will not let you be tested beyond your strength' (1 Corinthians 10.13), but Jesus is more merciful in this prayer. This is a prayer for safety, a prayer that we be spared the tragedies and atrocities that afflict so many in our world. It is a very honest prayer.

The version of the Lord's Prayer normally used adds a concluding clause, praising God to whom belong 'the kingdom, the power, and the glory'. This is not in the original text of the Gospels but is entirely in keeping with the prayer. It returns our focus to the kingdom that is present throughout the prayer. It also returns our attention to God, and from God takes confidence that the prayer will be heard and effective.

But beyond all of this, when we pray the Lord's Prayer we are taken to the Garden of Gethsemane, where Jesus prayed on the night he was arrested (Matthew 26.36–46; Mark 14.32–42; Luke 22.39–46; John 18.1–2). Here Jesus prays 'My Father, if it is possible, let this cup pass from me; yet not what I want but what you want' (Matthew 26.39). In the Garden of Gethsemane we see that Jesus' prayers were shaped in the same way that he taught his disciples to pray. We see him call on God his Father. We see him ask to be spared from the time of trial. We see him praying 'Your will be done'. And we see what the cost of living in the service of God's kingdom was for Jesus when we see him crucified. When we pray the Lord's Prayer we are praying the prayer Jesus taught us and we are praying in the way Jesus prayed. That is why the Lord's Prayer is so significant for Christians and why praying it is something Christians do every day.

The book of Revelation: the power of prayer

The last book of the Bible, Revelation, is often thought of as full of predictions and prophecies. But it may come as a surprise to learn that it is full of prayer and worship. Revelation is not primarily about predictions for the future. It is a book written to encourage and support Christians who are facing a time of trial. It speaks of the triumph of God and of the value of persevering as Christians. The first part of Revelation is taken up with letters to seven churches, offering warnings, encouragement and rebuke. Then John, the author and visionary, is taken through a door into heaven and into the heavenly throne room, where there is ceaseless prayer and worship.

An important way to read Revelation is to read it as a liturgy, an act of worship – it is peppered with hymns, songs and the language of worship. Revelation is full of worship and one of its important themes is the power of worship to offer us a window – or in Revelation's case a door – into heaven. Here we have a truer picture of reality than we have in our ordinary world – 'on earth'. Worship opens this door to heaven and places us in contact with God and the way the world is supposed to be. When we step out of worship we step out of heaven into a broken world. Worship offers us a vision of the world as it should be and also a vision of how things are going to be. If nothing else, the book of Revelation is an argument for the importance of prayer and worship.

As he goes through the door into heaven, John enters the place that all are invited to enter through the door of worship. Revelation does not contain a timetable for the end of the world; instead it offers these communities living under threat a different perspective. At the heart of the vision comes this song of prayer:

Great and amazing are your deeds,
    Lord God the Almighty!
Just and true are your ways,
    King of the nations!
Lord, who will not fear
    and glorify your name?
For you alone are holy.
    All nations will come
    and worship before you,
for your judgements have been revealed.
                (Revelation 15.3–5)

This is an invitation to God's people, to the persecuted communities to whom John first wrote and to Christians today – an invitation to worship God and to be given a foretaste of heaven. Prayer, according to Revelation, is a way into heaven that sends us back to earth strengthened in the service of God's kingdom.

The Psalms – the prayer book of the Bible

At the heart of the Bible sits the book of Psalms, which has been described as the prayer book of the Bible. There are 150 Psalms, arranged in five books. They are a crash course in praying. It has been said of the Psalms that 'all human life is there'. This was also the motto of the Sunday tabloid newspaper *News of the World*, famous for displaying some of the less savoury parts of human life. That could perhaps be said of the Psalms as well. I want to suggest four elements of the Psalms: praise, doubt, lament and vengeance. These do not exhaust the Psalms but they do give us some of the basic building blocks that make up the 150 prayers at the heart of the Bible.

An example of a Psalm of praise is Psalm 100.

Make a joyful noise to the LORD, all the earth.
    Worship the LORD with gladness;
    come into his presence with singing.

Know that the LORD is God.
    It is he that made us, and we are his;
    we are his people, and the sheep of his pasture.

Enter his gates with thanksgiving,
> and his courts with praise.
> Give thanks to him, bless his name.

For the LORD is good;
> his steadfast love endures for ever,
> and his faithfulness to all generations.

There is joy, thanksgiving and exuberance to this Psalm. It has been set to music many times and understandably so. In contrast, the aptly numbered Psalm 13 offers us doubt.

How long, O LORD? Will you forget me for ever?
> How long will you hide your face from me?
How long must I bear pain in my soul,
> and have sorrow in my heart all day long?
How long shall my enemy be exalted over me?

Consider and answer me, O LORD my God!
> Give light to my eyes, or I will sleep the sleep
> of death,
and my enemy will say, 'I have prevailed';
> my foes will rejoice because I am shaken.

But I trusted in your steadfast love;
> my heart shall rejoice in your salvation.
I will sing to the LORD,
> because he has dealt bountifully with me.

Here the repeated call of 'How long, O LORD?' displays frustration and even anger as the Psalmist tries to reconcile what is going on in life with the promises of God.

There is a deeper gloom to Psalm 120, which is an example of a Psalm of lament.

In my distress I cry to the LORD,
> that he may answer me:
'Deliver me, O LORD,
> from lying lips,
> from a deceitful tongue.'

What shall be given to you?
   And what more shall be done to you,
   you deceitful tongue?
A warrior's sharp arrows,
   with glowing coals of the broom tree!

Woe is me, that I am an alien in Meshech,
   that I must live among the tents of Kedar.
Too long have I had my dwelling
   among those who hate peace.
I am for peace;
   but when I speak,
   they are for war.

This is a Psalm of desperation, of not fitting in, of the dreadfulness of being a stranger and in the minority. A more troubling Psalm is Psalm 94, which begins and ends like this:

O LORD, you God of vengeance,
   you God of vengeance, shine forth!
Rise up, O judge of the earth;
   give to the proud what they deserve!
O LORD, how long shall the wicked,
   how long shall the wicked exult?

But the LORD has become my stronghold,
   and my God the rock of my refuge.
He will repay them for their iniquity
   and wipe them out for their wickedness;
   the LORD our God will wipe them out.
               (Psalm 94.1–3, 22–23)

This is strong stuff indeed. It is a call for God to get on and deal with things. It ends in confidence that God will destroy those the Psalmist dislikes.

Often the Psalms contain a mixture of all four of these basic elements. Psalm 69 starts as a mixture of doubt and lament. 'Save me, O God, for the waters have come up to my neck' (verse 1). It passes through vengeance, 'Let them be blotted out of the book of the living' (verse 28) and ends with praise: 'Let heaven and earth praise him, the seas and everything that moves in them' (verse 34). Psalm 69, like the book of Psalms, is a mixture of everything. This is not a cycle – like the cycle of grief – in which doubt yields to lament, which turns to vengeance before resolving into praise. The Psalms are not nearly so neat. The different elements pop up – at times unexpectedly – throughout the book of Psalms and sometimes within the same Psalm. It is all stirred up together, rather like life.

Some Psalms contrast the elements to make a point. Take, for example, Psalm 105. This is a long Psalm telling the story of the origins of the people of Israel. Starting with Abraham, it is a Psalm of praise in the form of a historical narrative. It tells the story of Joseph, sold into Egypt in captivity as a means of God saving his family. Then the Psalm continues with the story of Moses and the people of Israel leaving Egypt and being miraculously cared for in the wilderness. The highpoint is when it says that God did this out of faithfulness to his promise: 'For he remembered his holy promise, and Abraham, his servant' (Psalm 105.42). This Psalm needs to be read alongside the next one, Psalm 106, which also tells the story of Israel coming out of Egypt. However, Psalm 106 is a Psalm of lament in the form of a historical narrative. It laments the unfaithfulness of the people, from their rebellion at the Red Sea to the golden calf they made while Moses was receiving the Law from God. It concludes with a plea for God to restore Israel, 'gather us from among the nations, that we may give thanks to your holy name and glory in your praise' (Psalm 106.47).

Praise, doubt, lament and vengeance – these are the four basic elements of the Psalms. They do not exhaust the Psalms but rich seams of these elements can be found among them. However, in my experience at least, apart from when Psalms are used there are not rich seams of all of these in most gatherings for prayer and worship. There is a good deal of praise; little doubt (although it sneaks in from time to time). Lament is not something we are good at, making it harder for us to deal with times of tragedy. There is no mention of vengeance at all because we are trying to be good Christians and put on our Sunday best to go to church. What a contrast with the Psalms. The Psalms are raw prayer, without the filters we try to employ to make prayer more polite and safer. The Psalms are honest prayer. They have much to teach us.

The Psalms are not just examples of prayers to keep in the Bible. They are prayers to be prayed. In Jewish and Christian worship the Psalms are central. They are a staple part of the offices of Morning and Evening Prayer as they have developed in the Christian Church. The Book of Common Prayer suggests that the whole book of Psalms should be recited over the course of a month. This is broadly equivalent to saying five Psalms a day – not necessarily at the same time. Regular use of the Psalms as part of prayer is an excellent discipline. The Psalms need to be prayed.

The Bible in prayers

There are many prayers in the Bible. But the Bible has shaped and continues to shape the way Christians pray. A few years ago I came across a suggestions that to mark Bible Sunday churches should cut out of their services anything that came from the Bible. This was not a suggestion anyone expected to be taken up; it was to make the point that large swathes of worship comes, directly or indirectly, from the Bible.

Some parts of Christian worship are taken directly from the Bible. Aside from the actual reading of the Bible in worship (which is normally part of any service), we have already come across the Lord's Prayer and the Psalms. Another example would be the Magnificat, the song of Mary, which is said or sung every evening in many churches. It is one of a number of early Christian hymns that are found in the early parts of Luke's Gospel (in this case Luke 1.46–55), all of which are used regularly in Christian worship.

But the amount of worship that comes indirectly from the Bible is huge. Hymns and songs tell stories from the Bible, meditate on phrases from the Bible, rephrase the Psalms and use pictures and metaphors from the Bible. Prayers allude to Bible stories and use phrases from them. The more I know of the Bible, the more I see it being used in all kinds of ways in worship. It is a very interesting exercise to see just how much of any service depends on the Bible, one way or another.

Two phrases from the Psalms have come to shape a great deal of Christian praying. In one Psalm we find this verse: 'O LORD, open my lips, and my mouth will declare your praise' (Psalm 51.15). And in another Psalm we find this: 'Be pleased, O God, to deliver me. O LORD, make haste to help me!' (Psalm 70.1). These have become the opening sentences, said as a dialogue between service leader and congregation, in many services. They both express dependence on God for the worship to follow. The use of these verses in this way is very ancient and goes back to the earliest monks in the desert of Egypt in the fourth century. They are a simple and profound way in which the Bible has structured prayer and worship through the centuries and continues to do so today.

Praying with the Bible

The Bible contains many prayers and has shaped praying down through the ages. It is also something to be used in prayer. I want to introduce you to an ancient method of reading the Bible prayerfully called *lectio divina*, which means 'holy reading'. It dates to at least the sixth century but may well be older. The Psalmist writes that 'I will meditate on your precepts' (Psalm 119.15), and this is one way to take up what the Psalm suggests.

Lectio divina begins in silence and then reads a passage slowly and repeatedly. In this prayerful reading the aim is not to make historical or theological sense of the passage but to hear what God is saying through the Bible. It is a form of reading that can be done on your own or in a group. It is best to use a passage that is given to you, as a reading for the day or for the next Sunday. But any passage from the Bible can be used for *lectio divina*.

Here are some guidelines for using *lectio divina*:

Before reading
- Be still. Sit upright and comfortably. Uncross your arms and legs. Be silent and close your eyes.

First reading
- Read the passage through out loud and slowly. Listen for a word or phrase that stands out for you.

- Once the reading has finished, sit in silence for one or two minutes and repeat the word or phrase in your mind.

Second reading
- Read the passage through slowly again. Listen this time for why your word or phrase stood out for you.
- Once the reading has finished, say the word or phrase out loud.
- Sit in silence for one or two minutes and try to form a single sentence as to why this word stood out for you.

Third reading
- Read the passage through slowly again. Listen this time for what the word or phrase has to say to you.
- Once the reading has finished, sit in silence for one or two minutes and continue to listen for what God is saying to you through this word or phrase.
- If you are on your own, say a prayer of response to what God has said to you through this passage. Remember to be honest in your prayer!
- If you are doing this with others, you may want to share a little of what God is saying to each of you and then pray for one another.

Fourth reading
- Read the passage through a final time, and then sit in silence one more time.

Lectio divina is a very powerful way of reading the Bible. It flows from silence and returns into silence again. It needs no great knowledge of the Bible, nor a great intellect, but simply a humility to sit in silence and listen. 'Happy is the one who listens to me', says the Wisdom of God (Proverbs 8.34).

Try it out

1 Pick some Psalms at random and read them. What sort of prayers are they?
2 Try doing *lectio divina* using Matthew 11.2–6.

Further reading

Walter Brueggemann, *Praying the Psalms*, Winona, MN: St Mary's Press, 1982.

Stephen Cottrell, *Praying Through Life: How to Pray in the Home, at Work and in the Family*, London: Church House Publishing, 2003.

6

'In the beginning': creation in the Bible

Genesis was the world's first biology textbook.

Steve Jones[1]

One of the most important – and occasionally controversial – stories in the Bible is that of creation. In this chapter I'm going to look at three different stories about creation – about the way the world came to be. The first is from the Bible, Genesis 1.1—2.4. The second, pre-dating Genesis, comes from ancient Babylon and is called the *Enuma Elish*, from its first words meaning 'when on high'. The third is the story told by contemporary science, or at least a version of that story. Comparing these stories in some detail will give us a rich understanding of what creation in the Bible is about.

Please note that by talking about creation 'stories', wherever they are from, I don't mean to suggest they are not true. *How* they are true, or how they intended to be true, is at least as important as *whether* they are true. Terry Pratchett once wrote that 'All tribal myths are true, for a given value of "true".'[2] I think that is rather insightful. It enables us to ask what sort of truth these stories are trying to tell, to ask at a deep and fundamental level just what sort of stories are being told here. Each of the three stories needs to be interrogated, asked what 'value of "true" ' is being presupposed. Only then can we ask whether it has succeeded in being true.

So then to the stories. Are you sitting comfortably? Then I'll begin . . .

A first story: the seven days of creation

In the beginning when God began to create the heavens and earth, the earth was a formless void and darkness covered the face of the deep, while the Spirit of God swept over the face of the waters. Then God said, 'Let there be light' and there was light; and God saw that the light was good. And God separated the light from the darkness. God called the light day and the darkness he called night. And there was evening and morning, the first day.

The next day God said 'Let there be . . .' and it was so, and it was good. And there was evening and there was morning, the second day.

And the next day, and the next day, and the next day. God said 'Let there be' and it was so. And God saw that it was good, the third, the fourth, the fifth days.

On the sixth day, God said let us make people in our image, and let them have dominion over the other creatures. So God made people in his image, male and female. God blessed them and said, be fruitful and multiply, fill the earth, subdue it and have dominion over the other creatures. The plants are for your food, and for the food of the other animals. And it was so. And God looked at all he had made, and it was all very good. And there was evening, and there was morning, the sixth day.

On the seventh day, God finished the work he had done, and he rested. So God blessed the seventh day and made it holy because he rested on that day.

(Abridgement of Genesis 1.1—2.4)

What do we notice about this story? The first thing I notice is that it has a rhythm and a pattern to it. God speaks and it happens, and there is morning and evening, another day. It is constant, ordered, predictable and calm. There is something very methodical about the way the opening chapter of Genesis describes creation: day and night; earth and sky; land, sea and plants; sun, moon and stars; life in the sea; life on land (including human beings); rest. Seven stages, all ordered and in their proper place, and all arising from nothing more than God speaking. Nowhere does this feel like God shouting great commands over a soundtrack of thunder and dramatic music. Rather, it is a calmly spoken instruction, which then happens – 'And it was so'.

Related to this is the repeated refrain that 'God saw that it was good'. This too is something to notice about the story: it leaves us very clear that it considers the world and everything else to be good. The first thing God sees to be good is light, and from there the process of separation and making continues until on the sixth day God concludes that it was 'very good'. Within each stage there is reason for what is made: the separation of light and darkness produces day and night; the sun, moon and stars regulate the seasons; the creatures in the sea and on land are made according to their types; and, above all, human beings are given their roles. All is ordered, all is good – everything has its place and its purpose.

Finally we should notice the way the story ends not with a great climax of activity in making human beings but with rest. The story does not begin with nothing but it does end with nothing. God rests. God does nothing. Rather than being all about activity, the Genesis story is finally about rest.

Methodical, good, purpose, order from chaos, rest – these are the features of the Genesis account. But what sort of a story is it? What 'value of "true"' does it presuppose? The final assessment must wait until after we have looked at the other two stories, but for now let me say two things, one about a 'value of "true"' Genesis does use and one about a 'value of "true"' it does not.

First, the story of creation in Genesis is trying to establish that those features of its story – method, goodness, purpose, order over chaos, rest – are truly the values of creation. Some things, such as the practice of taking a day each week for rest, are explained by this story. Other things, such as the world and all that is in it being good, are assertions of a value. In the Genesis story the Bible is saying that the material world is essentially good. The biblical story goes on to explain how things go very badly wrong with this, but in the beginning things are good. When things go wrong they are tragic, not according to the design and need to be put right.

So one measure of truth in the Genesis story is that it is naming essential matters about the nature of the world. Method, goodness, purpose, order and rest are things that were built into the world when it was made. The second thing to say about this story concerns its historical claims. Are we to read this as meaning that the world came about in seven periods of 24 hours? Some would say 'yes'. There are Christians who fear that not to regard Genesis 1 as historically accurate would devalue the rest of the Bible. There are some atheists who agree, holding that Christians who don't regard Genesis 1 in this way have given up on their faith. But I don't think Genesis 1 should be read this way – and I haven't given up on faith. Historicity is not a 'value of "true" ' Genesis is trying to meet. The story knows itself to be telling truth in terms of its values and themes, but it is not trying to claim that everything was made in six days, followed by the Creator taking a well-earned day off. We will see this best when comparing the Genesis story to that of ancient Babylon.

A second story: war among the Gods (*the* Enuma Elish)

Before anything had a name, there was only Apsu, the sweet underground water, the begetter; and Tiamat, the salt seawater, mother of everything. As the waters of Apsu and Tiamat mingled, the gods were formed within them. The first Gods were Lahmu, the silt, and Lahamu, the mud.

The young gods gathered together and disturbed Tiamat as they moved and ran about. Apsu could not get them to be quiet. And what the young gods did was painful to them, their way was not good. Then Apsu, the begetter of the gods, went to see Tiamat. Apsu said to Tiamat, 'They have become painful to me, I have no rest and cannot sleep. I will destroy them and put an end to their way. Then we will have silence and can sleep.' When Tiamat heard this, she was angry and cried out to her husband 'Why should we destroy what we ourselves brought forth? Their way is painful, but let us be kind.'

When the gods heard this they sat in silence until Ea, the all-wise, devised a plan. He composed a spell on the water, pouring out sleep upon Apsu. He killed Apsu and from his body fashioned home. There he made his chamber and with his wife, he dwelt in splendour. Within Apsu, Marduk, the greatest of the gods, was born. Ea rejoiced and was filled with joy.

But some of the gods conspired with Tiamat their mother to avenge Apsu. Ea called Marduk to him. The gods gave Marduk the supreme place and made for him a throne over them all. Marduk went to battle. He caught Tiamat in his net, and as she opened her mouth to devour him, he drove the evil wind, the hurricane, into her throat so that she could not close her lips. Then, as the winds filled her body, he shot an arrow and it tore her apart, splitting her heart.

Then Marduk took the body of Tiamat and split it in two. Half of her he set in place to form the sky. He set guards and commanded them not to let the waters escape. From the other half he made the earth. He set up the stars and divided the year by constellations. He made the moon and entrusted the night to her.

The rebellious gods, who had marched with Tiamat, were enslaved and made to serve the gods. But in their distress they called out to Marduk for relief. As he listened to their words, Marduk resolved to create humans and impose on them the service that the gods now suffered. So Marduk called an assembly of the gods. 'Who was it', he asked, 'that caused Tiamat to rise against us?' 'It was Kingu,' they replied, 'Kingu who created the fight and made Tiamat rebel.' So they bound Kingu and took him to Ea, who cut his arteries. And from his blood Ea made humanity. He made them as slaves for the gods.

Then Marduk assigned the gods to guard his decrees. The gods praised Marduk. 'You have freed us from service,' they said, 'and as a mark of our gratitude we shall make a throne and make a dwelling for our rest in your honour.' And the gods made a sanctuary, which Marduk named Babylon, and at its heart was a shrine for Marduk. Then they praised Marduk, giving him 50 names. Marduk the avenger. Marduk whose commands are unbreakable. Marduk who ordered the heavens and the earth. Marduk who imposed servitude on those he had created and set free the gods.[3]

This is the Babylonian story of creation. It was told every Babylonian New Year. We have it written on seven clay tablets, found in Nineveh between 1902 and 1914, which date back to the seventh century BC. The story itself is older and may go back as far as the eighteenth century BC. Other fragments have been found, which have enabled the story to be restored almost in its entirety. It is written in cuneiform, one of the oldest forms of writing.

It is a story formed by a distinctive geography. Babylon is more or less where Iraq is today. And as we hear of Tiamat, the salt water, and Apsu, the fresh water, we are taken to the Persian Gulf. Where the River Tigris and the River Euphrates meet the sea there is an estuary. There the fresh water from underground and the sea water of the Gulf meet, and that commingling of the waters produces silt and mud. This story is rooted in the fertility of this part of the world, grounded in the experience of watching land created.

But leaving history and geography aside for now, what are we to make of the story? I want to ask the same three questions of the *Enuma Elish* that we asked of the Genesis story: What do we notice? What kind of truth is being offered here? How successful is it? Then we shall compare it to the story in Genesis 1.

The first thing we notice about the *Enuma Elish* is how violent a story it is. There are fights and murders, plots and wars, traps and schemes. Pretty much everything that happens in the story is as a result of violence. This is an epic to rival many a Hollywood film, with a body-count to match.

As you might expect, that means there is little plan to creation – it happens as a result of the destruction and fighting. Even the gods themselves seem to be the unintended consequence of the waters of Apsu and Tiamat mingling. Creation is an afterthought that Marduk has as he stands over the dead body of Tiamat – the world is made from the corpse of Tiamat. Appropriately for an afterthought, it is mentioned briefly in the story and then we move on to the next piece of action.

Human beings come out of the story a little better than the world: they are at least planned; but they are planned as a slave race, to allow the gods to be freed from service. They too are the result of violence, this time the execution of Kingu, the leader of the rebel gods. Humanity is made to be slaves.

With the creation of the world and the subsequent creation of human slaves taking such a little part of the story, one might ask whether this is really a creation story at all. Creation happens in it but the point seems to be to heap praise on the figure of Marduk. Nearly one and a half of the seven clay tablets on which the *Enuma Elish* is written are given over to the praise of Marduk's 50 names. The centre of the *Enuma Elish* is Marduk and his glory.

So we notice that this is a story full of and shaped by violence. Creation is unplanned, an afterthought fashioned from the debris of the fight. Human beings are made to be slaves. And the focus of the story is Marduk, the greatest of all the gods. What kind of truth, then, is the story offering?

The *Enuma Elish* offers two central truths. First, it tells us that the world is violent and that the power of the mighty – in combination with stealth, plotting and ruthlessness – is what makes things happen. The creation of human beings as slaves underlines the purpose of most people: to serve those who are mighty as gods. Slaves, who might be born in Babylon or taken in war, were made to serve the royal family, who styled themselves as gods.

The second truth of the *Enuma Elish*, the centrality of Marduk and his new home in Babylon (named by Marduk himself), points to the claims of Babylon to domination in the region. Babylon was indeed the seat of empire, becoming the religious centre of Mesopotamia under Hammurabi (1792–1750 BC). A millennium later, under King Nabopolassar (625–605 BC), it became a great empire reaching all the way around the Near East and taking in all of what is today Iraq, Syria, Jordan, Israel and Palestine and some of Iran, Saudi Arabia, Egypt and Turkey. Nabopolassar's son, Nebuchadnezzar II (604–561 BC), made Babylon into one of the wonders of the ancient world, building the Hanging Gardens and the great Ishtar Gate, through which each New Year, as the story of the *Enuma Elish* was told, statues of the gods were processed. Not for nothing did Saddam Hussein style himself as the 'Son of Nebuchadnezzar'.

And is it true? That is the question we must now ask. Having determined what kind of truths are proposed by the *Enuma Elish*, now we must ask whether they are successfully demonstrated. Can we believe them? The first truth that the story asks us to believe is that the world is a violent place in which the power of might rules. That may be true; it seems that there are many in the twenty-first century who believe it to be so. But the second truth the *Enuma Elish* tries to press upon us, that Babylon is the seat of the world empire, is certainly not true. In fact it is demonstrably false. In 539 BC the king of Persia, Cyrus the Great, conquered Babylon. His army diverted the river Euphrates, and while the city was still unaware his men marched in along the river bed. Babylon fell – the *Enuma Elish* cannot be true. Of course, this may just act as further evidence that it's first claim is indeed true.

Cyrus, who conquered Babylon, is something of a hero in the Old Testament, and especially for the prophet Isaiah. In Isaiah, God says of Cyrus 'He is my shepherd, and he shall carry out all my purpose' (Isaiah 44.28). 'Shepherd' is a term used for the leaders of Israel, and one verse later we read 'Thus says the LORD to his anointed, to Cyrus, whose right hand I have grasped to subdue nations before him and strip kings of their robes' (Isaiah 45.1). 'Anointed', in Hebrew, is *Messiah*! This is high praise indeed. But it may serve to remind us that the Old Testament was largely put together in exile in Babylon. In particular, the story of creation that we find in Genesis was written in Babylon.

The story in Genesis draws on the *Enuma Elish* in many different ways – here are some that we might notice. First, both are related to time. The *Enuma Elish* was read at the New Year festivities; the Genesis story is shaped on the week and offers the completeness of the week with a final day of rest. The violence and disorder of the *Enuma Elish* is countered by the peaceful and methodical way the Genesis story happens. The creation of the world is an afterthought for the *Enuma Elish*; for Genesis it is repeatedly described as 'good'. And above all, human beings are created as slaves in the Babylonian story, and this is used to justify the slavery that existed in Babylon. For the Israelite story, human beings are the pinnacle of creation, made in the image of God. To enslave such a being would be to enslave God.

It is not an exaggeration to say that the story of Genesis is consciously written to challenge and undermine the *Enuma Elish*. In particular, it is written to undermine the two central 'truths' of the

Babylonian story. The emphasis of Genesis on an orderly, peaceful creation directly contrasts with the violence of the *Enuma Elish*. But nowhere is the contrast and the undermining seen more than in the way the stories speak about the creation of human beings. The people of Israel in exile in Babylon were weak, enslaved in a foreign country. The New Year celebrations, and the story of the *Enuma Elish*, would have been part of the way they were told to understand their state. They were simply, like all human beings, made to serve Babylon and its gods. This has influenced the way the Genesis story speaks about the creation of human beings as made 'in the image of God' and created not as slaves but to have 'dominion' over all the other creatures. They are blessed by God and told to 'be fruitful and multiply'. And above all they are included in God's description of his creation as 'good' and 'very good'. The story told by the Israelite exile was told to undermine the story told by their captors. This is seen especially in the way the story of creation reaches its climax with God resting. Rest and silence was the ever elusive aim of the Babylonian gods. Apsu and Tiamat are disturbed by the younger gods, which is why Apsu plots to destroy them. In the end the gods can only achieve rest by creating human beings to be their slaves. In contrast, Genesis tells of a God who rests at the end of his creation, having made it to be free. God rests in the knowledge that all he has made is good, and God's rest has the effect of both blessing and creating the day of rest, the Sabbath, on which no work is done. Each week the Sabbath rest gave the exiles in Babylon a reminder that God made them for freedom, and made them with the dignity of those who are the image of God. The week is shaped to give hope and dignity to the weak!

All of this has the effect of denying the second truth the *Enuma Elish* is trying to establish – that Marduk is the greatest god and Babylon, his city, the seat of all power. Israel had been defeated in battle. Jerusalem had been destroyed and the Temple torn down. That should have been an end to Israel as a people and to their God as an object of faith. Israel's belief that the exile was a punishment for their unfaithfulness meant they could hold on to their faith and their identity even in the midst of exile in Babylon. It also had the effect of denying the greatness, even the existence, of the gods of Babylon.

They had not lost because Marduk had defeated the Lord, they had lost because the Lord used Babylon to punish them and teach them a lesson. The patient and peaceful ordering of creation Genesis 1 speaks about is simply another example of this all-powerful God at work. Marduk does not need to be defeated because he is simply irrelevant. It is God, and God alone, whose word brings forth life and who brings order from chaos.

We can see then that the truths the story in Genesis is trying to tell – that method, goodness, purpose, order over chaos and rest are the true values of creation – were hammered out against the background of slavery and exile. Genesis is engaged in a fight against the Babylonian story, which says that might is right. In the face of this, Genesis speaks of peace and order, goodness and rest. This can help us to see that these values are not self-evident (even in our world today); they are asserted in the face of the alternative view. Even when the view that might is right and the world basically a violent place seems to have more evidence going for it, Genesis quietly asserts a different truth.

Comparing Genesis 1 and the *Enuma Elish* also helps us to see the importance of the view of human beings in Genesis. For the Genesis story, human beings are created with care and imbued with dignity – they are not slaves. In the face of the *Enuma Elish* story that humans are created to be the slaves of the gods, and the reality of slavery experienced by the people of Israel in Babylon, this has an emphasis and importance that raises it to the level of another truth that the story in Genesis 1 is trying to convey. In Genesis all human beings are created by God – their dignity as human beings derives from being created by God and not from belonging to any other group, Babylonians, Israelites, believers or whatever. Human beings are created in the image of God before they have any other distinctions. The people of Israel, telling this story in exile in Babylon, included their captors in those made in God's image. Thus the Genesis story of human beings made in the image of God undermines all attempts to regard different people as having different values because of their class, clan, race, nationality, physical ability or anything else. It undermines attempts to place worth on different genders ('male and female he created them'). It has been instrumental in opposing and overturning slavery – Roger Ruston describes how the way Genesis 1 describes the creation of human beings became the foundation of modern human rights:

> The image of God doctrine delivers a belief in basic equality that would be very difficult, if not impossible, to arrive at by considering the secular reality of human life, with its multitude of ways in which human beings are ranged against each other on scales of value.[4]

So how successful are these truths demonstrated by the Genesis story? For a group of slaves in exile this truth claim must have been a matter of faith and hope. They were finally vindicated and returned home. That is why Isaiah celebrates Cyrus so much. But there is nothing obvious about the claims to peace and order that Genesis makes. It seems to have been written as an assertion that this way is true in the face of the evidence. In many ways Genesis seems to be calling for a decision that this is the right way against the Babylonian account of might makes right. It asks for our conversion to this truth.

A third story: a bang, growth and selection (contemporary science)

Take a proton.

There are about half a trillion of them in the ink in the dot of an 'i' – that's more than the number of seconds in half a million years in a tiny dot! Now shrink just one of those protons down to a billionth of its normal size. That's the space you have to cram in everything that there is. Every last particle of matter in the universe is now contained in a singularity. Now retire to a safe distance – except you can't: all of space is contained in the singularity. When the universe expands, it won't spread out to fill an empty space, it will create space as it goes. Nor can we ask how long the singularity is there for: all time is also contained in the singularity. Here, from nothing, from a singularity that contains all matter, all space and all time, here is where the universe begins.

'BANG!'

A single blinding pulse, too fast and too expansive for words, and the singularity expands. In the first second gravity and the laws of physics are produced. In this first second, scientific careers are made by shaving tiny fractions off how far back we can look. We can now, scientists claim, look back to the time 10^{-43} seconds after the bang – that's one ten million trillion trillion trillionths of a second. By the end of the first minute the universe is a million billion miles across. It's about 10 billion degrees Celsius as well, and nuclear reactions begin creating the elements, principally hydrogen and helium with a dash of lithium. By three minutes in, 98 per cent of all the matter there is or will be has been produced. All this was a long time ago, of course, about 13.7 billion years – although scientists reserve the right to argue about this figure, and most of the other ones as well. Since then the universe has grown a lot bigger, got a lot colder and a lot more complex. More complicated elements have formed.

This is, of course, a dead universe – or at least a universe with no life. For a universe to contain life all depends on the laws of physics, which were produced in the first second. Gravity, the mass of a proton and the density of matter need to be within some very precise ranges. In short, the universe needs to be like Baby Bear's porridge – 'just right'.

On at least one planet, ours, life has emerged. Here, in the uncharted backwaters of the unfashionable end of the universe, the conditions were such that molecules combined in a way that eventually led to proteins. Proteins became micro-organisms, and these tamed the planet, producing oxygen and an atmosphere. That in turn enabled more complex life and, step by slow, laborious and emergent step, many and varied forms of life began. Each lived in the conditions provided by the planet, and as the conditions changed, those forms of life best adapted to deal with them thrived, often at the expense of other forms of life. This 'natural selection' favours organisms that can make subtle changes that better adapt them to living in hostile circumstances. Evolution is ruthless.

Human beings form part of this enormous and evolving, seemingly random sequence. As the great apes evolved they grew more upright and developed larger brains. One of these apes left the forests of Africa and began to walk on the savannah. Gradually they began to walk upright. Their hands developed to enable them to throw things, and their enlarging brains allowed for strategy. They were still not human beings as we know them today – indeed at one point as many as six different types of hominid may have lived together in Africa. But the ruthlessness of evolution means that today there is only *Homo sapiens* – you and me.

Possibly the major human contribution to the story, other than massive levels of destruction, is that we bring a reflective consciousness to the party. So now we can have scientists who can tell us the story. But the story is not over. The processes of physics, chemistry, biology and evolution all continue, but now they are watched, and observation makes a difference.[5]

What do we notice about this third story? Perhaps the first thing to say is that this is a story full of numbers. That helps to lend it an air of precision, which is an important feature of the scientific account. The numbers themselves are fairly mind-numbing. I find a number that is the equivalent of more seconds than there are in half a million years pretty difficult to comprehend. Speaking of 13.7 billion years is almost impossible for me to grasp, and that's one of the lower numbers in this story (I suppose that technically 10^{-43} is the lowest number, but that's so small it feels like a really big number!). The precision and the immensity of numbers is a very significant feature of the scientific story.

Another thing to which the numbers contribute is a sense of history; that is, that there is a measurable timescale in which the events described happen. This is not a regular series but an attempt to be precise and to offer the real timeframe in which the events described in the story happened. Vast expense, both intellectual and monetary, is spent on the equipment and the experiments that establish the times of this story. The scientific story aims at being historical in that it claims to describe accurately the timescale of the story.

This in turn leads us to another feature of this story, which is that it is revisable and often in fact revised. The scientific story I have sketched is almost certainly untrue in that there has been further research that will have changed the view about many aspects of the story. The age of the universe is a number that has been revised many times and will no doubt be revised in the future. More fundamentally, when the account of the origin of the universe in a 'Big Bang' was first suggested, it was disputed – it remained a minority view for many years. Now, however, it is the accepted scientific orthodoxy. I say this not to dismiss the scientific story but simply to point out that the very nature of it is that it changes as knowledge changes. The great strength of it is that it can make use of the mistakes and puzzles that fall across its path.

A further feature of the scientific story is that it is a story able to include its own writing – the writing is itself something the scientific story can relate. The point of this story is to be able to account accurately for all that is. A failure to do so would lead to a revision of the story. Telling the story of how the scientific story is told is not just a matter of explaining the technology behind the computer and the software I have used to write this story. More than that, this story has to be able to account for the phenomenon of storytelling itself. The story told by science does not have an end – it continues and, at least in principle, would continue even were the human race to become extinct.

Mention of extinction points to another feature of the scientific story: it can seem very cruel. The physics at the root of the story speak of something called 'entropy', which is the sum total of disorder in the universe. Entropy only ever increases. In the singularity at the very start of the story, entropy is at a minimum. It has been downhill ever since – entropy increases relentlessly. One physicist once said that he felt a little guilty stirring his coffee because doing so added to entropy. When entropy rises to 100 per cent there will be no life at all. There will be no temperature. Everything will be cold and dead, the energy of the universe will all be uniformly distributed and there will be nothing to move energy from one place to another. Similarly Alfred, Lord Tennyson characterized Charles Darwin's theory of evolution, based on the survival of the fittest, as showing 'nature, red in tooth and claw'. Evolution works through extinction. If an adaptation evolves that is beneficial to a creature, the outcome will be that other varieties will die out. There is something fatalistic about the accounts of evolution and more generally, a seeming ruthlessness to the numbers involved in the scientific story. But this is not strictly true of the story. To speak of the story as 'cruel' or of processes and numbers as 'fatalistic' or 'ruthless' is to misinterpret them. It would be far better to speak of the 'indifference' of the whole story. Thousands may die, but the scientist has to record that and ask questions indifferently about precisely how many and the manner of death. Science is indifferent.

There is much in the scientific story to notice: numbers, history, revisions, self-involvement and indifference. Perhaps we should also notice the ease with which the story can be undermined, in its own terms, by being made to be 'about' something – humans, social policy or whatever. This is beginning to point us to the 'value[s] of "true"' being offered by this story. Clearly precision and accuracy are important. Equally important is the principle that the story must be changed – regularly and sometimes in a big way – if new evidence is found or a more compelling interpretation of the evidence is produced. Precision, accuracy and revision are, we should notice, not values aimed at the world beyond the story but rather at the way the story itself is told. The scientific story is to be accurate, precise, and needs changing to be told better. This speaks of perhaps the deepest value, the deepest truth, of the scientific story – that of indifference. The story told by science is not interested in anything other than itself, and telling that story better.

And how successful is the scientific story? How does it meet the 'value of "true"' it sets up? In one sense it is very successful – the story is as accurate as it can be, and its ability to be revised ensures it will get more and more accurate. If an inaccuracy can be identified and pointed out then it will be changed. At the same time, no individual telling of the story is true. My version of the story is therefore not the final version – far from it: it is at best a snapshot of where a debate stands. But within the scientific story that is a good thing – it contributes to the ongoing revision of the story and hence to its increasing accuracy.

How then does the scientific story compare to the story told by Genesis? We have seen that the Genesis story is not at all indifferent. It is written not to tell a revisable history but to hammer home the truth that human beings are worthy of dignity and freedom. In this respect Genesis comes from a completely different place from the scientific story. Genesis is written to oppose the *Enuma Elish* but it does not oppose the scientific story. In fact the regularity and goodness of creation of which Genesis constantly speaks, and which is utterly absent in the violent and haphazard creation in the *Enuma Elish*, has contributed to the ability of scientists to do science. In order to have any grasp on the world at all from a scientific perspective, what is required is an act of faith – faith that the world is in fact orderly and that this order can be found. The account of creation as orderly in Genesis, passed down through Jewish, Christian and – rather differently – Islamic thinkers, has enabled science to be written. Christians should rejoice in reading scientific accounts of the way the world has come to be, for they tell the same truths as the book of Genesis. Without the Genesis story, or something a lot like it, we might never have had scientists who thought there was order to be found, let alone who actually went out to find it!

So what then are we finally to make of the story in Genesis 1? It is not trying to offer a scientific or historical account of the first moments of the universe – that is one 'value of "true"' it is not trying to meet. Instead it is offering a robust account of a world that is ordered, good and purposeful: a world in which human beings are created with dignity and for freedom; a world in which all can and should have rest to enjoy the creation. These truths are stated by a people in exile; a people living in a world predicated on the chaos of violence, a world in which slavery is rife and rest unobtainable.

Is the story successful in establishing these truths? The existence of science, I have suggested, might be taken as evidence that the orderliness and goodness of creation has been established. Similarly, the existence of the Universal Declaration of Human Rights owes much to the notion of human beings as created in the image of God. Genesis has not finally abolished slavery or the poor treatment of human beings – a cursory glance at a news website should establish that. But it does offer a profound resource to challenge such crimes

and inhuman behaviour. To read Genesis 1 simply as a scientific state-
ment is to misread it badly, miss the riches it has to offer, and endanger
the voice of human liberation it contains.

Try it out

1 Read a book or a magazine that has a scientific focus.
2 Visit Amnesty International's website – <www.amnesty.org.uk> –
   and take an action to support human rights.

Further reading

Bill Bryson, *A Short History of Nearly Everything*, New York: Broadway
   Books, 2003.
Ellen van Wolde, *Stories of the Beginning: Genesis 1—11 and Other
   Creation Stories*, London: SCM Press, 1996.
The Universal Declaration of Human Rights (United Nations, 1948),
   available at <www.un.org/en/documents/udhr/index.shtml>.

7

Difficult subjects 1: money

———•◆•———

> There are three conversions necessary: the conversion of
> the heart, the mind and the purse.
>
> *Attributed to Martin Luther*

It may seem unlikely, but the Bible has a great deal to say about
money. In fact it turns out that money and economic issues are the
things the Bible has most to say about. What's more, economic issues
are not confined to one section of the Bible but can be found throughout it. Money is addressed as the Bible tells of the good gift of creation,
the freeing of people from slavery, rules for living as a community
in the Promised Land, the wisdom of the sages, the prayers of the
Psalms, the fierce criticism of the prophets, the stories of Jesus, the
letters of Paul and the vision of Revelation. Money is a constant theme
in the Bible.

Wealth and blessing and reward

The first thing to say about the Bible's teaching on money is that
it is not against material wealth. Indeed, material wealth is often a
sign of God's blessing. Noah is rewarded for his faithfulness and
godly ways, God saying to him 'I give you everything' (Genesis 9.3).
Jacob, not without his own brand of fixing, obtains the best of
the flock of his father-in-law and becomes rich. He attributes
this to a vision he received and tells his wives that 'God has taken
away the livestock of your father, and given them to me' (Genesis
31.9).

The life of the people of Israel in the Promised Land is also due
to be one of prosperity, provided they keep to God's laws. Deuteronomy
puts this the most clearly.

The LORD will make you abound in prosperity, in the fruit of your womb, in the fruit of your livestock, and in the fruit of your ground in the land that the LORD swore to your ancestors to give you. The LORD will open for you his rich storehouse, the heavens, to give the rain of your land in its season and to bless all your undertakings. You will lend to many nations, but you will not borrow. The LORD will make you the head, and not the tail; you shall be only at the top, and not at the bottom – if you obey the commandments of the LORD your God.

(Deuteronomy 28.11–13)

The Psalms say that those who fear the Lord 'will abide in prosperity' (Psalm 25.13) and the 'meek shall inherit the land, and delight in abundant prosperity' (Psalm 37.11). Even the prophets share this sense, and promise riches to God's people. Isaiah says that 'I will extend prosperity to her like a river, and the wealth of the nations like an overflowing stream' (Isaiah 66.12); and Jeremiah that 'I will heal them and reveal to them abundance of prosperity and security' (Jeremiah 33.6).

Wealth is a good thing, one of the blessings of God. This all derives from the goodness of creation. The created world is to be enjoyed; it is a gift from God. God says to the first human beings: 'See, I have given you every plant yielding seed that is upon the face of all the earth, and every tree with seed in its fruit; you shall have them for food' (Genesis 1.29). Creation is good, creation is to be enjoyed – this is the foundation for so much of the Bible's teaching. In the case of money and wealth, these are created things and so they are good – all material things, including material wealth, are gifts from God in creation and are therefore good. Prosperity is a blessing from God. It is also something that flows from following God's ways, and is thus a reward for those who are faithful.

The 'Prosperity Gospel'

One way the Bible's positive teaching about money and wealth has been misused is by those who take the Bible to say that those who are faithful to God and live in his way will be given everything for which they ask. Often called the 'Prosperity Gospel' or 'Name-it-and-claim-it theology', this approach builds on the theme of wealth as a sign of God's blessing and reward. Not only is wealth the sign of following God, but to be poor is a sign of God's rejection and punishment. Those who follow these teachers are encouraged to give, so that God can return more to them. In praying, the encouragement is to ask for material goods, even status symbols, and believe that God will give them to you. If you don't receive them, then you don't have enough faith.

There are all kinds of problems with the Prosperity Gospel as a form of Christian thinking; but it is also based on a poor reading of the Bible. The Bible certainly does teach that wealth is a blessing from God and a reward for following God's ways. But it does not teach that poverty is a sign of God's curse and a punishment for disobedience. The goodness of wealth and its blessings are only one side of the Bible's teaching. We next turn to a hugely important part of the Bible's teaching that completely undermines all that the Prosperity Gospel says – its account of the poor as precious to God.

The poor are precious to God

'Blessed are you who are poor', said Jesus (Luke 6.20), and in saying this expressed a huge theme within the Bible. The American pastor and activist Jim Wallis tells of how, in seminary, he and some friends took it upon themselves to identify every verse in the Bible that refers to the poor. They discovered that there were thousands. It was the second most frequent theme in the Old Testament after idolatry, and one in every 16 verses of the New Testament refers to the poor. One of the group took an old Bible and with a pair of scissors cut out every verse that referred to the poor.

> When the zealous seminarian was done with all his editorial cuts, that old Bible would hardly hold together, it was so sliced up. It was literally falling apart in our hands. What we had done was to create a Bible full of holes.[1]

With a theme that permeates the whole of the Bible, God's care for the poor can be found in all kinds of biblical literature. The books of the Law contain many laws for the people of Israel based on the care of the poor. They are not to reap the edges of their fields, but to leave them for the poor (Leviticus 23.22). They are to take care that lawsuits are fair to the poor (Exodus 23.6). Alternative sacrifices are prescribed for the poor to offer (Leviticus 12.8 – Jesus' parents offer this cheaper sacrifice in Luke 2.24), and the wages of the poor are to be paid promptly (Deuteronomy 24.14–15).

The Psalms also refer to the poor. They warn of the wicked who 'persecute the poor' (Psalm 10.2), and 'draw the sword and bend their bows to bring down the poor and needy' (Psalm 37.14). However, 'the needy shall not always be forgotten, nor the hope of the poor perish for ever' (Psalm 9.18) since ' "Because the poor are despoiled, because the needy groan, I will now rise up," says the LORD' (Psalm 12.5). 'The LORD maintains the cause of the needy, and executes justice for the poor' (Psalm 140.12) and the king, likewise, is to 'defend the cause of the poor' (Psalm 72.4). For the Psalms, treatment of the poor is part of faithfulness to God. Similar themes can be found in Proverbs, which also condemns those who do not care for the poor: 'Those who oppress the poor insult their Maker'; 'Those who mock the poor insult their Maker' (Proverbs 14.31; 17.5). Conversely, those who are generous are praised: 'happy are those who are kind to the poor' (Proverbs 14.21); 'Whoever is kind to the poor lends to the LORD, and will be repaid in full' (Proverbs 19.17).

This care for the poor is taken to a new level in the prophets. Amos rails against the people of Israel who are involved in 'buying the poor for silver and the needy for a pair of sandals' (Amos 8.6). Isaiah sees God judging his people and asking 'What do you mean by crushing my people, by grinding the face of the poor?' (Isaiah 3.15). Jeremiah tells the people of Judah that 'on your skirts is found the lifeblood of the innocent poor' (Jeremiah 2.34). Zechariah could stand for all the prophets when he gives the instruction 'do not oppress the widow, the orphan, the alien, or the poor' (Zechariah 7.10).

In the New Testament this theme is still there. Not only was Jesus born to a family too poor to offer the prescribed sacrifice, but he spent much of his ministry with the poor and the outsiders. He linked this to the prophetic visions, telling John the Baptist's disciples that 'the blind receive their sight, the lame walk, the lepers are cleansed, the deaf hear, the dead are raised, and the poor have good news brought to them' (Matthew 11.5, quoting Isaiah 61.1). The same passage from Isaiah is used to introduce his ministry in Luke's Gospel. Jesus reads from Isaiah that 'The spirit of the Lord is upon me, because he has anointed me to bring good news to the poor' and then tells his hearers: 'Today this scripture has been fulfilled in your hearing' (Luke 4.18, 21). Elsewhere Paul makes a collection for the poor of Jerusalem, describing himself as 'eager' to 'remember the poor' as the elders in Jerusalem had instructed him (Galatians 2.10) and James says that God has 'chosen the poor in the world to be rich in faith and to be heirs of the kingdom' (James 2.5).

This is a rich vein of biblical teaching, showing remarkable tenacity throughout the time during which the Bible was written and consistency across the range of authors and genres within it. If it is ignored by the proponents of the so-called Prosperity Gospel, then it has become a major plank in the teaching of Liberation Theology. This is a movement born in Latin America among Roman Catholic priests ministering in poor rural communities and shanty towns. Its understanding of God's 'preferential option for the poor' has clearly had some influence on the life and teaching of Pope Francis. While this movement has been dismissed by critics as relying too much on Marxist analysis, it should be clear that it has a deep biblical grounding for its emphasis on the poor. No reader of the Bible can miss the biblical concern for the poor – it is a major theme found throughout the whole of it. To read the Bible without noticing the poor is to fail to see one of its main threads.

Justice in dealings

Alongside this emphasis on the poor, indeed almost as a result of it, the Bible teaches that justice is important. Sometimes there is a straightforward emphasis on fair dealing and honest trading, such as in the proverb that 'A false balance is an abomination to the Lord, but an accurate weight is his delight' (Proverbs 11.1). This means that a bias to the poor is not acceptable. 'You shall not render an unjust judgement; you shall not be partial to the poor or defer to the great: with justice you shall judge your neighbour' (Leviticus 19.15). Nevertheless, the Bible recognizes that 'the oppression of the poor and the violation of justice and right' (Ecclesiastes 5.8) often go together. The judgement of God sits over all of this, especially to preserve justice for the poor.

There is particular condemnation for those whose wealth is obtained as a result of oppressing the poor. The prophet Micah describes these as 'the treasures of wickedness' derived from a 'scant measure' (Micah 6.10). Jeremiah also condemns those who:

> take over the goods of others. Like fowlers they set a trap; they catch human beings. Like a cage full of birds, their houses are full of treachery; therefore they have become great and rich, they have grown fat and sleek. They know no limits in deeds of wickedness; they do not judge with justice the cause of the orphan, to make it prosper, and they do not defend the rights of the needy. (Jeremiah 5.26–28)

Amos, never one to mince his words, has God refusing worship because of the injustice that his people commit:

> I hate, I despise your festivals, and I take no delight in your solemn assemblies. Even though you offer me your burnt-offerings and grain-offerings, I will not accept them; and the offerings of well-being of your fatted animals I will not look upon. Take away from me the noise of your songs; I will not listen to the melody of your harps. But let justice roll down like waters, and righteousness like an ever-flowing stream. (Amos 5.21–24)

Even the kings of Israel do not escape this criticism. David's adultery and subsequent killing of Bathsheba's husband are described by the prophet Nathan in terms of a rich man who 'was loath to take one of his own flock or herd to prepare for the wayfarer who had come to him, but he took the poor man's lamb' (2 Samuel 12.4). When David expresses righteous anger at the injustice, he is skewered by the story – Nathan tells him 'You are the man!' (2 Samuel 12.7). Much later in Israel's history, King Ahab tries to buy a vineyard from Naboth the Jezreelite that is next to the royal palace. When Naboth refuses to sell, Ahab's wife Jezebel has Naboth judicially murdered and his lands confiscated. God sends Elijah with the message that 'you have sold yourself to do what is evil in the sight of the LORD' (1 Kings 21.20).

In the New Testament the story of Zacchaeus is one of unjust wealth given away. Zacchaeus is a chief tax-collector, and owed his wealth to fraud and bullying. Yet after hosting Jesus he repents and declares that 'half of my possessions, Lord, I will give to the poor; and if I have defrauded anyone of anything, I will pay back four times as much.' Only then does Jesus declare 'Today salvation has come to this house' (Luke 19.8–9).

The book of Revelation contains a long denunciation of 'Babylon' (which is really Rome) in which the city is described as a harlot, dressed in jewels and indulging in all kinds of luxuries. John, recounting his vision, lists all the things that he sees:

> gold, silver, jewels and pearls, fine linen, purple, silk and scarlet, all kinds of scented wood, all articles of ivory, all articles of costly wood, bronze, iron, and marble, cinnamon, spice, incense, myrrh, frankincense, wine, olive oil, choice flour and wheat, cattle and sheep, horses and chariots, slaves – and human lives.
>
> (Revelation 18.12–13)

The cost of this luxury is paid ultimately by human beings. Those who mourn for Babylon (Rome) are the merchants who 'have grown rich from the power of her luxury' (Revelation 18.3). Rome, whose wealth is founded upon the desires of the rich and on 'slaves and human lives' is judged and cast down.

Paying interest

So far we have seen that the Bible regards wealth as a reward and a blessing, but also sees the poor as precious to God. It is thus very clear that God stands against those who gain their wealth from unjust means. One very specific piece of economic teaching that can be found in the Bible is that interest is not to be charged. 'If you lend money to my people, to the poor among you, you shall not deal with them as a creditor; you shall not exact interest from them' (Exodus 22.25). Here it is clear that loans are not a normal feature of life, but only used when someone falls into hardship. The law is clear that the misfortune of others is not to be used as an opportunity for making a profit. Similar sentiments are found in Leviticus.

If any of your kin fall into difficulty and become dependent on you, you shall support them; they shall live with you as though resident aliens. Do not take interest in advance or otherwise make a profit from them, but fear your God; let them live with you. You shall not lend them your money at interest taken in advance, or provide them food at a profit.

(Leviticus 25.35–37)

The danger of allowing debts to mount up, leading to people never being free of the financial hold of another, produced the year of Jubilee – a year in which all debts were cancelled and all had the opportunity to start with a clean balance sheet (Leviticus 25).

The prophet Ezekiel lists taking 'advance or accrued interest' among those things that the righteous will refuse and the iniquitous will do (Ezekiel 18.8, 13, 17; 22.12). Nehemiah complains to the nobles and officials that 'You are all taking interest from your own people' (Nehemiah 5.7). The Psalms count those 'who do not lend money at interest' (Psalm 15.5) as among the blameless. Jesus exhorts his disciples to 'lend, expecting nothing in return' (Luke 6.35).

The prohibition on charging interest is one of the clearest teachings of the Bible on money. It was observed widely until the sixteenth century. Theologically, the teaching of the Protestant reformer John Calvin began to permit the charging of interest with very tight conditions. However, these conditions were largely ignored and interest became a regular part of the financial world. The world's economy today is run on interest-bearing debt, affecting both individuals and whole nations. It is clear that this has greatest affects on the poorest, again both individuals and nations. Whether it is the role of debt in penalizing poor countries or the cost of pay-day loans, perhaps there is something in the biblical approach to which we need to pay attention.

Money as a spiritual issue

The Bible says so much about money because money has a profound impact on human lives. That makes money a spiritual issue. The first letter to Timothy warns that:

those who want to be rich fall into temptation and are trapped
by many senseless and harmful desires that plunge people into
ruin and destruction. For the love of money is a root of all kinds
of evil, and in their eagerness to be rich some have wandered
away from the faith and pierced themselves with many pains.

(1 Timothy 6.9–10)

Money has an effect on human desires, and that may lead us into
doing things we might not otherwise do. Desiring wealth or money
over other things distorts human life. The first letter to Timothy
suggests a better way: 'there is great gain in godliness combined with
contentment; for we brought nothing into the world, so that we can
take nothing out of it; but if we have food and clothing, we will be
content with these' (1 Timothy 6.6–8).

Jim Wallis and his seminary class discovered that the poor were the
second most frequently mentioned theme in the Old Testament –
as we noted above, only idolatry is mentioned more often, and the
two are sometimes related. Ahab, whose taking of Naboth's vineyard
enraged Elijah, is also described as one who 'acted most abominably
in going after idols' (1 Kings 21.26). The prophets complain that
the poor are oppressed and also that the people have worshipped
false gods. Hosea speaks of Israel as 'A trader, in whose hands are
false balances' and complains that 'they keep on sinning and make
a cast image for themselves, idols of silver made according to their
understanding' (Hosea 12.7; 13.2).

Idolatry is the worship of something that is not God. An idol, a
carved or cast figure that becomes the object of worship, is a material
thing. It is part of God's creation and to worship it is to mistake the
creature for the Creator. To worship something material is to distort
ourselves. It is a fruitless quest to find ultimate meaning in something
that has been made. The biblical emphasis on the goodness of creation is a means of warning people against this fruitless and distorting
path. When the first letter to Timothy speaks of 'the love of money'
there are definite overtones of idolatry. To love money is to love
something that cannot bear our love and will ultimately fail to return
our love. In the meantime our love of money will distort us and lead
us to do things that are damaging to ourselves and to others.

Money and wealth are part of God's gift in creation and therefore they are good. However, they are particularly dangerous in that they all too easily become focuses of love and worship. Jesus himself warns that 'No one can serve two masters; for a slave will either hate the one and love the other, or be devoted to the one and despise the other. You cannot serve God and wealth' (Matthew 6.24). The word 'wealth' here is perhaps better left untranslated so that Jesus' saying becomes 'you cannot serve God and Mammon'. Mammon, the Aramaic word for 'riches', has been personified into a god, a rival master to God. Instead, Jesus teaches his disciples: 'Do not store up for yourselves treasures on earth . . . For where your treasure is, there your heart will be also' (Matthew 6.19, 21). Paul also warns against 'greed (which is idolatry)' (Colossians 3.5).

Just because something is good does not mean it cannot be turned to harm. Indeed, it is only because something is good that it can exert the hold on us that distorts our being and does us such damage. This is the insight of the biblical warning against idolatry. It is something that seems to be particularly true of money and its capacity to mould and shape us. Jesus' warnings that we cannot serve God and Mammon find a contemporary echo in the work of Peter Selby. He writes that 'as money has increased in its quantity and volatility it has more and more acquired the capacity, as the idols of old did, to transform human desires.'[2] Selby catalogues how money has changed our society and even the Church, so that it distorts the good and damages people.

Living with money

With such dire warnings ringing in our ears, we may find ourselves asking the same question as Jesus' disciples. Jesus has told a man that all he must do is to 'go, sell what you own, and give the money to the poor'. The man sadly leaves, 'for he had many possessions', and Jesus turns to his disciples and tells them 'How hard it will be for those who have wealth to enter the kingdom of God!' The disciples are astounded and say to one another 'Then who can be saved?' (Mark 10.17–27).

The key biblical teaching is not to be ruled by money, not to live as though money were our creator and master instead of God. Care for the poor will be an essential part of this. So will acting justly and not looking for gain at the expense of others. But let me suggest two further biblical means by which we may help ourselves avoid the idolatry of money. The first is generosity. The first letter to Timothy, having warned against the idolatry that is the love of money, continues with a more positive approach for those who have money.

> As for those who in the present age are rich, command them not to be haughty, or to set their hopes on the uncertainty of riches, but rather on God who richly provides us with everything for our enjoyment. They are to do good, to be rich in good works, generous, and ready to share, thus storing up for themselves the treasure of a good foundation for the future, so that they may take hold of the life that really is life.
>
> (1 Timothy 6.17–19)

Generosity points us beyond our riches, to the generosity of God.

The other practice is that of thankfulness. So important is thankfulness that the Bible commands that the people of Israel mark three harvest festivals.

> Three times a year all your males shall appear before the LORD your God at the place that he will choose: at the festival of unleavened bread, at the festival of weeks, and at the festival of booths. They shall not appear before the LORD empty-handed; all shall give as they are able, according to the blessing of the LORD your God that he has given you.
>
> (Deuteronomy 16.16–17)

Paul's letters are dotted with thanksgiving and instruction that those he wrote to should do the same. He tells the Christians in Colossae that 'whatever you do, in word or deed, do everything in the name of the Lord Jesus, giving thanks to God the Father through him' (Colossians 3.17); and those at Thessalonica are instructed to 'give thanks in all circumstances' (1 Thessalonians 5.18). All rests on what God has already given us: 'Thanks be to God for his indescribable gift!' (2 Corinthians 9.15).

Between them, thanksgiving and generosity work to undermine the idolatrous power of money. They loosen our hold on money and remind us that it comes to us as a gift of God in creation. In giving thanks we are reminded that money and wealth are good things, part of God's good creation. In giving generously we are reminded that we are to care for the poor and not to hold on to created things for their own sake. They come together in a prayer of King David: 'all things come from you, and of your own have we given you' (1 Chronicles 29.14). This is how the Bible would have us handle money.

Try it out

1 Look for ways to be thankful for all that you have.
2 Do something generous today.

Further reading

Ben Witherington III, *Jesus and Money: A Guide for Times of Financial Crisis*, London: SPCK, 2010.

8

Difficult subjects 2: sex

———•◆•———

God is sexy.
Jo Ind[1]

The Bible has much less to say about sex than it does about money.
This is worth remembering when confronted by another media report
about sex and the Church. Sex remains, however, an important theme
in the Bible. It is important because it is crucial to human relationships. It is also important because it offers clues to the possibility of
relationship with God.

Sex is good

There is no better place to start an account of sex in the Bible than
with the Song of Songs. This is a work of erotic love poetry, attributed
to King Solomon. Its opening verses, which I remember from a 1980s
pop song, read like this:

> Let him kiss me with the kisses of his mouth!
> For your love is better than wine,
>   your anointing oils are fragrant,
> your name is perfume poured out;
>   therefore the maidens love you.
> Draw me after you, let us make haste.
>   The king has brought me into his chambers.
> We will exult and rejoice in you;
>   we will extol your love more than wine;
>   rightly do they love you.
>
> (Song of Songs 1.2–4)

Here there is kissing, oil for rubbing into bodies and perfume to
enchant the senses. There are maidens who also fancy the beloved;

perhaps this is why there is haste to make love. This is a poem of love, delight and joy. It is, not to put too fine a point on it, sexy.

There are many similarities between the Song of Songs and Arab wedding songs from Syria. Some of the imagery of the Song still resonates as love poetry in our culture. When the man is described as like 'a young stag on the cleft mountains' (Song of Songs 2.17) or when the woman says that 'I arose to open to my beloved, and my hands dripped with myrrh, my fingers with liquid myrrh, upon the handles of the bolt' (5.5), we can still understand the imagery. Other imagery is more obscure. When we read that 'Your hair is like a flock of goats, moving down the slopes of Gilead. Your teeth are like a flock of shorn ewes that have come up from the washing . . . your two breasts are like two fawns' (4.1–2, 5), we may not even guess whether a man or a woman is being described until we come to the reference to her breasts!

Right at the heart of the Bible we find this love poetry. It is testimony only to the strength of love and makes no ethical demands. The Song is only interested in the love that the lovers share. It revels and rejoices in their lovemaking; sharing the joy and sorrows that flow from their love. Love and sex are entwined in the Song. The poem contains expressions of longing and desire as well as descriptions of the beauty of both woman and man. It also contains the pain of parting and the fear of losing the beloved: 'I sought him, but did not find him; I called him, but he gave no answer' (5.6). It also contains one of the deepest and most passionate descriptions of love in any language:

> Set me as a seal upon your heart,
>   as a seal upon your arm;
> for love is strong as death,
>   passion fierce as the grave.
> Its flashes are flashes of fire,
>   a raging flame.
> Many waters cannot quench love,
>   neither can floods drown it.
> If one offered for love
>   all the wealth of one's house,
>   it would be utterly scorned.
>   (Song of Songs 8.6–7)

This is a book that recounts a longing for the physical presence of the lover. 'O that his left hand were under my head, and that his right hand embraced me!' (8.3). Nothing in the Song of Songs is spiritualized, God is never mentioned. From start to finish it describes desire and longing. The urgency of the beginning is still there at the end of the book. 'Make haste, my beloved, and be like a gazelle or a young stag upon the mountains of spices!' (8.14).

This is a remarkable book of the Bible but not an uncontroversial one. The rabbis argued over its inclusion. One rabbinic saying suggested that anyone who sang the Song of Songs in a banquet house would have no share in the world to come, but Rabbi Akiva, who died in AD 135, declared that the whole world was not worth the day in which the Song of Songs was given to Israel, 'for all the scriptures are holy, but the Song of Songs is the Holy of Holies'.[2] The rabbis came to see the Song as referring to the love of God for Israel. In a similar fashion Christians came to see it as referring to the love of Christ for his Church. There are medieval commentaries on it that are some of the greatest Christian works on prayer. These ancient interpretations are probably responsible for the Song remaining part of the Bible.

None of this detracts from the intense eroticism of the poem. Much of the Song is spoken in the voice of a woman, making it even more unusual in the Bible. There is nothing coercive about the sex in the Song; there is no duty or demand, just longing and love. The vineyard, a key metaphor in the Song, belongs to the woman. 'My vineyard, my very own, is for myself' (8.12). Her body, her love, her sexuality is for her to give to whom she chooses. Sex is clearly good, according to the Song of Songs; and good sex is physical, sensual, urgent, full of desire and loving. Importantly, it is also consensual and given freely. It may then be an image of God's love for us.

Sex in creation

If sex is good then it too goes back to the goodness of all creation. Here we find the story of a man being all alone.

Then the LORD God said, 'It is not good that the man (*adam*) should be alone; I will make him a helper as his partner.' So out of the ground the LORD God formed every animal of the field and every bird of the air, and brought them to the man (*adam*) to see what he would call them; and whatever the man (*adam*) called each living creature, that was its name. The man (*adam*) gave names to all cattle, and to the birds of the air, and to every animal of the field; but for the man (*adam*) there was not found a helper as his partner. So the LORD God caused a deep sleep to fall upon the man (*adam*), and he slept; then he took one of his ribs and closed up its place with flesh. And the rib that the LORD God had taken from the man (*adam*) he made into a woman and brought her to the man (*adam*). Then the man (*adam*) said, 'This at last is bone of my bones and flesh of my flesh; this one shall be called Woman (*ishshah*), for out of Man (*ish*) this one was taken.' Therefore a man leaves his father and his mother and clings to his wife, and they become one flesh. And the man and his wife were both naked, and were not ashamed.　　　　　　　　　　　　(Genesis 2.18–25)

Here, just as in the Song of Songs, we notice a lack of compulsion. There is something of a beauty parade going on, as God leads the different creatures to Adam to name them and to see if they will be able to counter his loneliness and be his helper and partner. The freedom of Adam to choose which will be his partner is essential to the story. God does nothing to pressure Adam to choose any of the creatures.

This story also tells of the origins of the differences between men and women. The story begins with 'the man', for which the Hebrew word *adam* is used. Once the woman has been created, the man (*adam*) speaks for the first time and uses the words 'woman' (*ishshah*) and 'man' (*ish*). Some ancient commentators suggest that the man (*adam*) was androgynous until the arrival of woman. The first creation story in Genesis describes the difference between the genders as there from the start. 'God created humankind (*adam*) in his image, in the image of God he created them; male and female he created them' (Genesis 1.27). Again, we see *adam* being used for all human

99

beings, and male and female as subsets of this humanity. The differences between men and women are needed to give full expression to being human, to being in the image of God.

We must handle this account of the image of God carefully lest it lead to the understanding that only couplings of men and women can show the image of God. Single people, or even married people apart from their spouses, also display the image of God. More dangerously, we should resist the idea that there is sexual differentiation within God. God does not have a gender. We can refer to God as 'Father' or as 'Mother' – both can be found in the Bible but these are not properly understood to be claims about the gender of God! When the book of Genesis says that human beings, male and female, show the image of God, it is not a mathematical formula for identifying God's image (man + woman = image of God). Rather it is a broader point that both men and women display the image of God; the image of God does not belong to one gender alone. Nor can any individual claim to be the image of God, because God's image is seen in all human beings. These negative claims are important because they undermine claims to power over others. More positively, the creation of all people in the image of God shows the value of all human life and the infinite creativity of God.

The delight that we saw in the Song of Songs is also present in the story of Adam. When Adam does choose, his reaction is one of joy – at last, the right person to be with! There is delight and no shame or fear. There is nothing to be ashamed of in their difference and in the joy they take in one another. This is childlike delight. One commentator compares it to 'toddlers splashing in a paddling pool'.[3] This is a clear contrast to the eroticism of the Song of Songs.

What we have in the creation stories is an account of human sexuality that is not forced but chosen freely. It is an account in which both men and women in their differences show the image of God. Here in the Garden, human sexuality is joyous, unashamed and without fear. It is here that the Genesis story locates the origin of marriage. It comes from delight and lacks shame and fear. It is not a duty or an obligation but springs from the beauty parade God offers to Adam.

Sex and marriage

Marriage is the next major theme in the Bible's understanding of sex. It is rooted in the creation story and specifically in the unforced choice of Adam to have a partner and helper and the delight of recognition when that partner is found. The themes of freedom from coercion, partnership, reflecting God's image and delight are all to be focused through the married relationship. Notice as well that in marriage 'a man leaves his father and his mother and clings to his wife, and they become one flesh' (Genesis 2.24). There is eroticism here in the clinging to one another, but the main force is the becoming 'one flesh' – not an erotic image, this is rather one of kinship. In marriage a couple become something new, a new family. Marriage is about more than a coupling for sex, it involves becoming related to one another, forging a new 'flesh and blood' relationship recognized by others. That is why it also involves leaving existing families – it is about starting a new family.

Among its many functions, marriage is also the location for sex. Sex belongs to the marriage relationship. This is mostly established in the negative. Perhaps the best example of this is the commandment, 'You shall not commit adultery' (Exodus 20.14), but notice also the final commandment, 'you shall not covet your neighbour's wife' (v. 17). The Ten Commandments are the core of the Torah and express some of the basic requirements for living as a people. We can take from this that the marriage partnership is an important building block for the creation of human society and that this involves faithfulness within marriage. Marriage is a place for disciplining sex so that it can be the free partnership of delight it is meant to be.

Most important of all, however, is to see the commandment forbidding adultery in the context of the first commandment that 'you shall have no other gods before me' (Exodus 20.3). The exclusive nature of marriage stands under and is related to the exclusive nature of the relationship of God and his people. When God's people turn away from him, this is often described in terms of adultery – almost the whole of the book of Hosea is taken up with this image. As with the ancient interpretations of the Song of Songs, albeit in a very different style, human sexual relationships offer insight into relationship with God.

This use of marriage to express relationship with God is taken up as a metaphor for how God will restore creation. Isaiah's vision of the restoration of God's people is described in terms of a marriage.

> You shall no more be termed forsaken, and your land shall no more be termed Desolate; but you shall be called My Delight Is in Her, and your land Married; for the LORD delights in you, and your land shall be married. For as a young man marries a young woman, so shall your builder marry you, and as the bridegroom rejoices over the bride, so shall your God rejoice over you. (Isaiah 62.4–5)

The same imagery is used in the book of Revelation:

> Halleluiah! For the Lord our God the Almighty reigns. Let us exult and give him the glory, for the marriage of the Lamb has come, and his bride has made herself ready . . . Blessed are those who are invited to the marriage supper of the Lamb.
> (Revelation 19.6–7, 9)

Jesus also makes use of this metaphor. When he turns water into wine at a wedding in Cana, the Gospel calls this the 'first of his signs' (John 2.11). It is a sign that this marriage of God and his people is at last to be celebrated. Many of Jesus' parables are set at weddings, and this image of the marriage of God and his people is behind this as well.

Marriage is the primary way the Bible talks about sex. Marriage is the exclusive relationship in which sex can enable the couple and even wider society to flourish. It is founded in the free choice of partner and the delight of the creation stories. With the ancient interpretations of the Song of Songs, marriage speaks of the passionate love and commitment of God to his people, so much so that it is one of the most important images of the new creation found in both the Old and the New Testament.

Some difficulties

This picture of sex and marriage in the Bible is not, however, the full picture. The Bible speaks of them in some difficult and troubling ways and there are changes to the understanding of marriage through-out the period during which it was written. This creates enough tension, but changes in the long period since the Bible was written also cause problems in understanding what it has to say about sex and marriage. We must now look at five of these difficult areas.

Equality and subordination

Our exploration of difficult areas begins by returning to the Ten Commandments. In the midst of the command to faithfulness in marriage, and the way this echoes the faithfulness of God and his people, we find that the tenth commandment ranks coveting a neighbour's wife alongside coveting slaves, animals and belongings. In short, it regards coveting a wife as a property offence. This affected the way the commandment not to commit adultery was understood. Either man or woman could commit adultery but who they offended against was understood differently. Were the woman to commit adultery, she offended against her husband. But were it to be the man, then he has offended against the husband or father of the woman with whom he has sex. This is a long way from equality.

Subordination remains an issue in the New Testament. The first letter to Timothy uses the order of creation and the story of Eve tempted by the serpent as a reason to forbid women from teaching (1 Timothy 2.11–15), apparently unconcerned that this was Adam's – unsuccessful – defence as well (Genesis 3.12). Paul picks up the image of marriage as a means of speaking of God's relation with his people and uses it to apply to Christ and the Church. However, he also uses it to justify the subordination of wives in marriage. 'Wives, be subject to your husbands as you are to the Lord. For the husband is the head of the wife just as Christ is the head of the church' (Ephesians 5.22–23).

There is some evidence that these passages from the Bible are used to justify violence towards women. We seem to have moved a long way from the helper and partner of Genesis, and from the free choice of Adam and of the woman in the Song of Songs. If we are to retain the joy and freedom of a biblical approach to sex and marriage, we need also to be very critical of the subordination of women when we find it.

Polygamy

The stories from Genesis and the poetry of the Song of Songs seem to imply that monogamy is the pattern for married life. However, that was far from the case for much of the Old Testament. In fact the Bible is remarkably short of examples of monogamous marriages that can be described as straightforward. Abraham and most of his male descendants had multiple wives – Jacob was perhaps the most extravagant, with four wives. All this pales before the marital arrangements of King Solomon: 'Among his wives were seven hundred princesses and three hundred concubines' (1 Kings 11.3). When the Book of Common Prayer marriage service looks to commend examples of married life in the Bible, the only one it can come up with is that of Isaac and Rebecca. (Their parenting skills, however, are not such a good example!)

Polygamy was always the preserve of the rich in Israel, mostly of the king. Again it shows us the inequality of relationship between man and woman, and again there are signs that it views women as property. By the time of the New Testament, however, it appears that monogamous marriage was the norm. The long-term influence of the story of Adam in Genesis 2 may be a contributory factor to this. Most significantly, what we see in the shift from polygamy to monogamy within the Bible is evidence of a changing understanding of marriage. Marriage is simply not an unchanging institution over the course of the time in which the Bible was written. Nor has it remained unchanged since then.

Celibacy

Paul was not a great fan of marriage. He was single, and while perfectly happy for those in his churches to be married, thought that the better option was to remain single: 'I wish that all were as I myself am' (1 Corinthians 7.7). Paul's reasons for preferring celibacy seem to have been that it could be a distraction from the work of the gospel and lead to suffering in the coming crisis. Marriage was a state for those who could not manage to stay celibate, 'it is better to marry than to be aflame with passion' (1 Corinthians 7.9), or for those who were already married when they became Christians.

When added to the fact that Jesus never married, this makes for a strong case for celibacy at the very origin of Christianity. The early Church made much of virginity as a state of holiness. This was particularly the case for women, who found in celibacy an honoured state that preserved them from the subordination of marriage and the dangers of childbirth. Celibacy was a liberating option for women. In the face of a culture that is so sexualized, and by which so much damage is inflicted on people, might there yet be a case for celibacy as a liberating place for both men and women? It remains an honoured Christian approach to sex and marriage.

Divorce

The Old Testament certainly permits divorce.

> Suppose a man enters into marriage with a woman, but she does not please him because he finds something objectionable about her, and so he writes her a certificate of divorce, puts it in her hand, and sends her out of his house; she then leaves his house and goes off to become another man's wife. Then suppose the second man dislikes her, writes her a bill of divorce, puts it in her hand, and sends her out of his house (or the second man who married her dies); her first husband, who sent her away, is not permitted to take her again to be his wife after she has been defiled; for that would be abhorrent to the LORD, and you shall not bring guilt on the land that the LORD your God is giving you as a possession.   (Deuteronomy 24.1–4)

It will be immediately apparent that this is entirely at the whim of the male party. No sufficient reason has to be given, and a wife can simply be dismissed. Read more closely, this passage can be seen as an attempt to regulate the practice of divorce so that some care has to be taken for the wife. The clear implication is that another husband has been found, so that she is not left destitute. That does not much soften what is otherwise a very hard state of affairs.

By the time of the prophet Malachi, perhaps with the influence of the sense that marriage was a sign of God's relationship with his people, divorce is viewed much less favourably. 'I hate divorce, says the LORD the God of Israel ... So take heed to yourself and do not be faithless' (Malachi 2.16). Jesus' approach appears to be in the same vein. He views the permission of divorce in Deuteronomy as a concession to 'your hardness of heart' (Mark 10.5). Instead, 'Whoever divorces his wife and marries another commits adultery against her; and if she divorces her husband and marries another, she commits adultery' (Mark 10.11–12). This position is softened in Matthew's Gospel, where an exception for unfaithfulness is made (Matthew 19.9).

Divorce is clearly unwelcome in the Bible's account of marriage. It does not meet the high standards of forming a new family, nor does it witness to the faithfulness and love of God for his people. Yet there is also a recognition that it happens. Paul has to deal with new Christians who are married to pagans. He counsels that in so far as they have any say, they should remain married. However, he accepts that this will not always be the case, and 'if the unbelieving partner separates, let it be so' (1 Corinthians 7.15). Divorce is always a failure of relationship, and painful for that. While recognizing that lifelong faithful relationships are the standard at which marriages should aim, the Bible is also witness to the grace of God in starting afresh, and accepting us where we are.

Same-sex marriage

On the five occasions when the Bible mentions homosexuality, Leviticus 18.22; 20.13; Romans 1.26–27; 1 Corinthians 6.9; 1 Timothy 1.10), it regards it as wrong. The reason for this stems largely from its place in the holiness code in Leviticus. 'You shall not lie with a male as with a woman; it is an abomination' (Leviticus 18.22). There continues to be argument among scholars about whether faithful and committed same-sex relationships are referred to in these texts, or would even have been within the experience of the biblical writers. In fact the argument has become so political that it is now almost completely unproductive.

What is clear is that there is a change in the social arrangements in some parts of the world to permit same-sex marriage. We have seen that the Bible contains different accounts of marriage, which follow societal moves from permitting polygamy to an insistence on monogamy. We have seen the accommodation of divorce within the Bible, despite its contradiction of the best standards that the Bible knows. We have seen the danger within the Bible of accounts of women as property and as subordinate to men. How then should we respond to the introduction of same-sex marriage?

One clear advantage of same-sex marriage is that it can help us to see better the equality of marriage. In a marriage in which there is no male to be superior, or one in which there is no female to be subordinate, the equality of the partners is much more clearly visible. It could be that same-sex marriage can actually improve all marriage. It may also be the case that Paul's teaching that 'it is better to marry than to be aflame with passion' (1 Corinthians 7.9) proves a source of accommodation. Given that Paul sees marriage itself as an accommodation to human weakness, this is good pastoral advice for anyone. We could take this as being a step to allowing those who are 'aflame with passion' for those of the same sex to take a better path in their discipleship.

The real question, it seems to me, is whether we can see holiness in the lives of married same-sex couples. This is the very thing that is disputed by Leviticus and taken up by the New Testament writers. My suggestion through this account of marriage in the Bible has been that the holiness of marriage can be seen in a number of ways. It can be seen in the free choice of commitment, just as Adam was given a free choice of partner. It can be seen in the joy and delight of the partnership, as Adam delights in Eve and as the couple in the Song of Songs delight in one another. It can be seen in the witness of the relationship to the faithful love of God, as we see in the interpretation of the Song and in the visions of the new creation. If we can see these things in same-sex marriages, then they are holy indeed!

Try it out

1 Play your favourite love song. Can you sing it as a song to God?
2 What examples of good relationships can you find in the Bible?

Further reading

Rob Bell, *Sex God: Exploring the Endless Connections Between Sexuality and Spirituality*, Grand Rapids, MI: Zondervan, 2007.

Adrian Thatcher, *Liberating Sex: A Christian Sexual Theology*, London: SPCK, 1993.

9

Difficult subjects 3: violence and the Bible

Bring night to your imaginings. Bring the darkest passage
of your holy book.

Carolyn Forché[1]

Here we turn to some of the darkest stories of the Bible. Violence is
a pretty constant theme – from Cain and Abel to the war in Revelation
preceding the new creation, violence is always there. On many occasions the violence can be seen as the effects of the sin of Act 2 of our
six-act play (see Chapter 3). This shows the Bible recording wrongdoing but not supporting it. There are some passages, however, with
which it is much harder to reckon. Chief among these is a story in which
the prophet Samuel gives a command of God to King Saul that he
should attack the Amelekites and utterly destroy them (1 Samuel 15).
No one is to be spared, no man, woman or child, not any livestock.
This has the effect of removing the spoils of battle for the victorious
Israelites, and they ignore this command. Saul in particular, perhaps
mindful of his own position, spares Agag, the king of Amelek. The
next day, having had a vision in which God says he regrets having
made Saul king, Samuel turns up. He can hear the bleating of sheep
and chastises Saul for his disobedience. Samuel kills the king of
Amelek and informs Saul that God has rejected him as king. It is
a horrific story.

For me this is the most difficult passage of the whole Bible. It
has God complaining that Saul has not massacred every living thing
in Amelek. I know the background to this story; I know that the
Amelekites opposed Israel when they came out of Egypt, causing God
to vow that they would be blotted out (Exodus 17.8–16); I know that
the rules of holy war stated that nothing would be taken as spoil but

all destroyed; I know as well that the first book of Samuel is full of Samuel's angst that there should be a king in Israel at all. But none of this can take away the difficulty of this passage, of God's command to kill and his anger when Saul didn't complete the massacre.

I hope that my sense of moral outrage over this chapter is shared – I really do. I want to return to it, and I hope that it continues to burn. First, however, I want to look at two other places in which violence and death are part of the Bible. Then I want to look at some possible ways of reading the Bible that might help with this problem. Only then will I return to 1 Samuel 15 and try to suggest how I read a Bible that contains such a horrific story.

Cursing verses in the Psalms

We have seen that vengeance is part of the praying contained in the Psalms. At times this cry for vengeance runs very deep and the Psalms pray for harm to come to others. In some prayer books these verses are printed in brackets, as a sign that they might not be said. They have become known as the 'cursing verses', and they stand in the central work of prayer in the Bible.

Perhaps the most well known of these cursing verses is found in Psalm 137. This is a Psalm that tells of the pain of exile in Babylon: 'By the rivers of Babylon – there we sat down and wept when we remembered Zion' (v. 1). The Psalm records the taunts of captors, asking the exiles to sing songs from home. And the Psalm ends in fury and vengeance.

> Remember, O LORD, against the Edomites
>   the day of Jerusalem's fall,
> how they said 'Tear it down! Tear it down!
>   Down to its foundations!'
> O daughter Babylon, you devastator!
>   Happy shall they be who pay you back
>   what you have done to us!
> Happy shall they be who take your little ones
>   and dash them against the rock!
>   (Psalm 137.7–9)

This is strong stuff indeed.

Cursing verses are found elsewhere in the book of Psalms. Some further examples are:

> Let death come upon them;
> let them go down alive to Sheol;
> for evil is in their homes and in their hearts.
>
> (Psalm 55.15)

> O God, break the teeth in their mouths.
>
> (Psalm 58.6)

> Let them be blotted out of the book of the living;
> let them not be enrolled among the righteous.
>
> (Psalm .69.28)

> May his days be few;
>   may another seize his position.
> May his children be orphans,
>   and his wife a widow.
> May his children wander about and beg;
>   may they be driven out of the ruins they inhabit.
>
> (Psalm 109.8–10)

There are more cursing verses should you wish to find them. Some ask God that people will come to physical harm, some ask God for people to die, some ask for consequences to be felt by the children of their enemy. These are not polite prayers!

There is a way of reading these verses that suggests that they are about a general hatred of evil that is personified into these very specific requests about harm to befall an enemy. Who would not wish the teeth of evil broken? Who would want the children of evil to prosper? In so far as these verses can be read in very general terms, this is a perfectly fine way of reading them and making them useful as prayers. Perhaps we would do better if we were more visceral in our opposition to evil. But even granting that this approach can be useful, I am not convinced it does away with the fact that some at least of the cursing verses were meant originally as vengeance against enemies. Some if not all of these prayers for violent retribution were exactly what they seem.

A more fruitful way of understanding the cursing verses might be to examine the honesty in prayer that they embody. I have never heard prayers in a church – other than these verses from the Psalms – that call for harm to come to other people. That need not be the only indicator of honest prayer. But too often our prayers do not go very deep in bringing our true feelings before God. We may be lucky enough that we cannot relate to situations in which evil appears to have triumphed, but I strongly suspect that most people can relate to the feelings of the Psalmist when he or she asks for vengeance. Where the Psalmist differs from me – at least – is in bringing the feelings of hatred and vengeance to God in prayer.

This I think is the most constructive approach to the cursing verses. They give us an insight into truly honest prayer, prayer that can even bring the darkest of our desires before God. By reading and praying the cursing verses we are encouraged to open the darkest parts of ourselves in prayer to God. We are people who seek revenge. We are people who have the capacity for violence. The Psalms recognize this and their honesty about it enables us to be honest about ourselves before God. It is also perhaps worth noting that these verbal pleas for vengeance and violence are simply that – verbal. Expressing these aspects of ourselves honestly and openly to God does not mean we will go and do acts of violence. Indeed, being honest about the desire may help us refrain from such acts. Asking God to take vengeance for us is, if nothing else, a handing over of our retaliation to God. It is an end to our vengeance. If the cursing verses do nothing other than encourage us to be more honest in prayer and more honest about ourselves, then they are worth their challenging place in the Bible.

Anti-Semitism in the Gospels?

If the cursing verses show us violence at the heart of the Bible's prayer book, then we must now examine a charge of anti-Semitism at the heart of the story of Jesus. In the stories of Jesus before Pilate, the Gospel writers place great emphasis on the guilt borne by the Jewish people. Matthew records Pilate saying '"I am innocent of this man's blood; see to it yourselves." Then the people as a whole answered, "His blood be on us and on our children"' (Matthew 27.24–25). Here the Jewish people are referred to as 'the people as a whole' and seem to agree with Pilate that he is – however inaccurately – innocent.

John's Gospel also uses the story of Jesus before Pilate as the occasion to have the Jewish people say words by which they condemn themselves. 'From then on Pilate tried to release him, but the Jews cried out, "If you release this man, you are no friend of the emperor. Everyone who claims to be a king sets himself against the emperor"' (John 19.12). Here John suggests that the Jews are giving up their Messiah (king) to the Romans for execution.

The first thing to say is that these verses have been used to 'justify' anti-Semitism. The passage from Matthew, in particular, has led to many major and minor instances of persecution of Jews by Christians. This is abhorrent and wrong. It is also wrong interpretation of the Gospels. Perhaps the best way of illustrating this is by a consideration of the three contexts that we saw in Chapter 2. In this I will look primarily at Matthew, but similar things could also be said of John.

The first context is that of the writer, and here we can say clearly that Matthew was a Jew writing for Jewish Christians. This seems clear from reading his Gospel. Whatever this passage is about, it cannot be a simple denunciation of all Jewish people. We don't know where Matthew was writing, but he does reflect a time of tension between non-Christian Jews and Jewish Christians. Throughout his Gospel he refers to 'their synagogues', and it would seem likely that Matthew was writing at a time when Jewish Christians had been expelled from synagogues, at least in the place in which Matthew was writing. This was part of what came to be a definitive parting of the ways between Judaism and Christianity. Matthew is writing at a time of tension but before the parting was permanent. If there is persecution in the context in which Matthew is writing, it is of Jewish Christians by non-Christian Jews.

The second context is that of the wider book. The passage itself seems best understood as part of an explanation for why Jerusalem was destroyed by the Romans in AD 70. This, for Matthew at least, is seen as a tragedy that needs to be understood. He sees in the rejection of Jesus by so many of his fellow Jews an explanation of why God has allowed the destruction of the city. To take this passage as some kind of justification for persecuting Jews is to ignore all kinds of material in the rest of the Gospel. Jesus is himself Jewish, descended from Abraham and David (Matthew 1.1–18); he urges his disciples to 'Love your enemies and pray for those who persecute you' (5.44); he tells a Gentile woman that he was 'sent only to the lost sheep of the house of Israel' (15.24); and quotes Jewish Scripture as he dies (27.46, quoting Psalm 22.1). Matthew's Gospel offers no real grounds for persecution of any sort, least of all anti-Semitism.

The absence of the grounds for persecution in either the first or second context makes the third context, the context in which we read the Bible, so important. We as readers inherit the history of the use of this passage to justify persecution. We are formed by the history of Christian persecution of Jews which turned to these passages for support. More recently our history tells of the attempted genocide of the Jewish people in Nazi Germany. We live in a world where anti-Semitic violence remains a threat to Jewish people across the world. All of this is part of how we read the passage today. In this third context we read a text that has been contaminated and discoloured by its use in history. It is incumbent upon us as readers to recognize this, to take responsibility for the way we read the passage and to ensure that it is not used in this way again.

It is not the case that the Gospels are anti-Semitic. They do say things about Jesus that Judaism would not agree with but they are written by Jews (except in the case of Luke) for an audience that certainly included Jews (and in the case of Matthew was probably largely Jewish). Above all they are about a Jew – Jesus. But we cannot read the Gospels today without being aware that they have been used, however badly and ignorantly, to justify anti-Semitism. Anyone reading the Gospels must be aware of this history and read in such a way that it is not allowed to happen again.

Facing the violence in the Bible

Many writers have tried to offer ways around or through the difficulties of the violence that is contained in the Bible. It is worth outlining the strategies employed by four writers in particular.

Regina Schwartz – the problem of monotheism

Perhaps, in the face of the violent stories in the Bible, we should either do away with the Bible or radically change its nature. That is the contention of Regina Schwartz. She identifies the basic problem as being monotheism. The Bible promotes the worship of one God, and that leads necessarily to the – often violent – exclusion of all other gods. Thus Schwartz speaks of 'the bloodiness of exclusive monotheism'.[2] Schwartz argues that violence originates in the way we form our identities. We identify ourselves by excluding others. This form of creating identities is something she identifies with monotheism, and the enormous cultural impact of the Bible has been to form identity in this way for believers and non-believers alike. The only way to escape from the violence of monotheism is to jettison monotheism and allow a variety of gods to hold our allegiance. In the service of this vision she advocates not rejecting the Bible but opening it to new stories and new myths, creating 'a Bible embracing multiplicity instead of monotheism'.[3]

Schwartz's solution to the problem of violence in the Bible is to reject the Bible, at least to reject it in its present state. That is an option, and one it is important to consider, but not one I would advocate. Schwartz's rejection of monotheism, as described by the Bible, doesn't really consider what biblical monotheism replaced. The Old Testament condemns the worship of Molech, who demanded the sacrifice of children. Leviticus includes a command prohibiting the worship of Molech in the name of the one God: 'You shall not give any of your offspring to sacrifice them to Molech, and so profane the name of your God: I am the LORD' (Leviticus 18.21). For children facing sacrifice to this god, biblical monotheism looks far less violent than the alternative. Schwartz holds us to the problem of violence but cannot provide a way through it. Nevertheless her suggestion of abandoning the Bible as it is remains the only option unless an alternative way through can be found.

Phyllis Trible – texts of terror

One such alternative that explicitly holds on to the Bible while finding it horrific is that of Phyllis Trible. Trible speaks of 'Ancient tales of terror [that] speak all too frighteningly of the present'.[4] Trible tells four terrible stories, without pulling her punches. She does so because these stories are part of the Bible and so part of the stories in which believers live. She also does so because they can speak to us of things that might otherwise be forgotten. So the story of Hagar, Sarah's slave girl given to Abraham and then sent away into the wilderness (Genesis 16.1–16; 21.9–21), is told because 'all sorts of rejected women find their stories in her'.[5] Similarly, the story of an unnamed woman (Judges 19.1–30) who is betrayed, raped, tortured, murdered and dismembered concludes with the recognition that misogyny leads to the death of women. This is a very contemporary issue. According to Women's Aid, two women a week in the UK are murdered by a current or former male partner. Trible ends her account of the woman's story with the call 'Repent. Repent.'[6]

This approach to texts of terror is helpful in a number of ways. It allows us to be honest that these texts are indeed terrible, and not to read them looking for piety and deeper meanings. It forces us to confront the violent and terrible stories and in doing so confront violence and terror in our own world. And it recognizes that any attempt to exclude violence from the Bible would remove the possibility for many people suffering violence and terror of finding meaning in the Bible. This is a hard but important path to tread through these stories. Trible finds the story for this path in the story of Jacob wrestling with an angel. 'To tell and hear tales of terror is to wrestle demons in the night, without a compassionate God to save us.'[7] Trible urges us to wrestle, to hold on and to seek a blessing from even the most terrible passages.

Marc Ellis – concentric reading

Marc Ellis is a Jewish theologian heavily influenced by Christian Liberation Theology. His proposal draws upon Jewish traditions of concentric reading. In this method of reading, the Torah stands at the centre and is read through the remainder of the Hebrew Bible, the Talmud and other commentaries. Reading continues through a host of other ongoing interpretations, arguments and questions. Recognizing that, as we have seen, the Christian Gospels have been used to justify anti-Semitism, and also that the Jewish stories of the Exodus and the Promised Land have been used to justify the dispossession of Palestinian land, Ellis proposes that we add stories of atrocity to the use of the Bible in worship. This will add an important layer to the concentric reading of the Bible.

> For Christians, the gospel of Matthew is now to be read along-side the gospel of Treblinka; for Jews the book of Exodus will be complemented by the book of Palestine. With the reading of the history of the community alongside the holy texts – as an expanded and evolving new canon – the core of the tradition is refocused from a pretended innocence to a tradition in struggle with its own culpability.[8]

Ellis goes on to suggest that there are other stories of atrocity – slavery, apartheid – that could and should be read alongside the religious texts that justify them.

There is much to commend Ellis' idea. Indeed, the Bible itself supports this method – although Ellis does not say this. The stories of the kings of Israel act as commentary on the way God's people live out the commandments. The Acts of the Apostles shows how the Church acts on the teaching of Jesus. Ellis' proposal may intensify this but it is in line with the Bible's own approach. In the approach to reading the Bible I am suggesting, the use and abuse of the Bible to justify atrocity is an essential part of the third context for reading. I might add that many Christian traditions, at least in the UK, mark Holocaust Memorial Day on 27 January with services of penitence and commitment in which stories are told and the memory of the Holocaust and other genocides is preserved. That is coming close, I think, to Ellis' proposal of concentric reading.

René Girard – the victim's perspective

A French writer, René Girard, has written more than anyone else on the way the Bible interacts with violence. Girard reads the Bible alongside other accounts of religion. He notices many similarities, not least in the role violence plays in the origins of communities. So Cain, the first murderer, builds the first city; the origins of the people of Israel come as they are expelled from Egypt; Christianity begins with the crucifixion of Jesus. What is different about the Bible,

Girard claims, is that it tells the story from the point of view of the victim. Compare the story of Cain and Abel with the story of Romulus and Remus. Both tell the story of the founding of a city and both involve the founder of the city killing his brother. But the Bible tells the story of Cain and Abel in order to show that Cain does wrong whereas the story of Romulus and Remus is told to glorify the founding of Rome. This biblical emphasis on the victim is supremely seen in the stories of the crucifixion of Jesus.

Girard goes further than this. He suggests that it is the biblical revelation of the truth of the victim that enables us to view our culture critically. 'I propose that if today we are capable of breaking down and analysing cultural mechanisms, it is because of the indirect and unperceived but formidably constraining influence of the Judaeo-Christian scriptures.'[9] This cultural impact of the Bible enables this critical approach to our culture whether or not we are Christians, Jews or even believers. The Bible even gives us the vocabulary to articulate how people are persecuted. We often speak of innocent people or groups being 'scapegoated' – the word 'scapegoat' only entered the English language when William Tyndale translated the Bible!

How then should we read?

At the heart of the New Testament, and at the heart of the Bible, there is an act of violence – the tortuous death of an innocent man, condemned by a combination of political and religious leadership. Crucifixion was an act considered so shameful that there are very few written accounts of it in ancient literature. Yet at the heart of the Christian faith is a book that contains four fairly detailed and graphic accounts of crucifixion, and letters that all allude to it. If violence is one of the themes of the Bible, then this is where it all reaches something of a climax. The centrality of the crucifixion of Jesus means that we cannot have the Bible without violence. To do so would be to excise the very heart of biblical teaching. It strikes me that only people who have experienced nothing but peace and prosperity would ask for a Bible without violence. For those who have encountered violence and oppression, the fact that the Bible contains accounts of violence is what enables it to speak.

So let us return to 1 Samuel 15, our horrific story. How can we read a Bible that contains this horror? Let us begin, with the Psalms, by recognizing that we are people capable of violence and revenge. It is not good enough to express horror at this horrific story in such a way that makes it sound as if it were something completely beyond human experience. The Psalms, with their reminder of our personal capacity for violence and revenge, will not allow this. If nothing else, there is a truthfulness to the Bible in recording that violence is such a common human capacity.

It is important also to read the stories of the Bible in context, as we saw in Chapter 2 and in reading the much misused verses of the Gospel accounts of Jesus' death. The third context, that of the contemporary world in which we read, is very important in reading 1 Samuel 15. By looking at this context we can see that claims to divinely sanctioned genocide are still with us. Again, at the very least the Bible records this hard truth about human behaviour.

The truthfulness of speaking of such horrors is the reason to read the story in 1 Samuel, however hard this may be. Phyllis Trible's approach to texts of terror urges us to wrestle with the story, holding on until it yields a blessing. This is also my tenth 'commandment' for Bible reading in Chapter 1. Marc Ellis' suggestion of concentric reading would have us place contemporary atrocities alongside this story. Both are helpful approaches. What they do is to increase the horror of the story by showing us how terrible it really is.

What is vitally important is to ask where our horror at this story comes from. I am assuming that readers of this story find it horrific, and fear for the humanity of anyone who does not find it so. Why do we find this story so horrific? If there is any truth to Girard's work then, at least in part, it comes from the influence of the Bible. The reason I find 1 Samuel 15 such a horrific story is that I am so deeply formed by the story of Jesus and the crucifixion of an innocent man. It turns out that it is the Bible that teaches me that parts of the Bible are texts of terror and stories of horror.

In reading and wrestling with the Bible it is important to be honest. Effective wrestling with the Bible can only happen if we are honest that we find some bits difficult and even horrific. That is all right. For me, as I confronted this story, I had to hold on, wrestle until morning, and find that there was blessing in the Bible itself showing how horrific was the story it contained.

Try it out

1 What is the most difficult part of the Bible for you? Why?
2 What helps you hold on as you wrestle with terrible stories?

Further reading

James Alison, *Knowing Jesus*, London: SPCK, 2012.
Jürgen Moltmann, *The Crucified God: The Cross of Christ as the Foundation and Criticism of Christian Theology*, 2nd edn, trans. R. A. Wilson and John Bowden, London: SCM Press, 2001.

10

'Eat this book': the Bible in our lives

———•◦•———

> It is a mistake to look to the Bible to close a discussion;
> the Bible seeks to open one.
>
> *William Sloane Coffin*[1]

Our tour of the Bible, and how to read it, is nearly over. However, the Bible will not let us go quite so easily. It is, as we have seen, many things: a book made up of many books; a conversation; a long story comprised of many other stories; and containing difficult and dark passages. But to describe the Bible from the outside is not enough, at least not for the Bible itself. For the Bible also makes demands on us. Its dark passages are often challenges to our understanding and our way of life. Its story, and its stories, wants to include our own stories. It is a conversation that invites us to join in. It is a book that asks us to eat it.

Sweet and sour

On two occasions in the Bible a prophet is commanded to eat a book. The first is the prophet Ezekiel, when he hears a voice speaking to him in a vision.

> But you, mortal, hear what I say to you; do not be rebellious like that rebellious house; open your mouth and eat what I give you. I looked, and a hand was stretched out to me, and a written scroll was in it. He spread it before me; it had writing on the front and on the back, and written on it were words of lamentation and mourning and woe. He said to me, O mortal, eat what is offered to you; eat this scroll, and go, speak to the house of Israel. So I opened my mouth, and he gave me the scroll to eat. He said to me, Mortal, eat this scroll that I give you and

121

fill your stomach with it. Then I ate it; and in my mouth it was
as sweet as honey.   (Ezekiel 2.8—3.3)

For Ezekiel, although the scroll contains difficult and troubling words,
it is nevertheless sweet in his mouth.

A similar thing happens to John, the visionary of the book of
Revelation.

> Then the voice that I had heard from heaven spoke to me
> again, saying, 'Go, take the scroll that is open in the hand of the
> angel who is standing on the sea and on the land.' So I went to
> the angel and told him to give me the little scroll; and he said
> to me, 'Take it, and eat; it will be bitter to your stomach, but
> sweet as honey in your mouth.' So I took the little scroll from
> the hand of the angel and ate it; it was sweet as honey in my
> mouth, but when I had eaten it, my stomach was made bitter.
>   (Revelation 10.8–10)

For John, like Ezekiel, the scroll is sweet in his mouth. But it is more
difficult to digest, proving bitter in his stomach.

Both Ezekiel and John are instructed to do more than speak
the words of God. They are instructed to eat them, to find in those
words nourishment and to take those words into themselves where
they can be built into the fibre of their very beings. These stories of
eating scrolls are not just visionary excess, they are a way of describing how the Bible intends to be more than words, however good
those words may be. The Bible intends to become part of our lives.

Both the book of Ezekiel and the book of Revelation are riven
with allusion to other parts of the Bible. The sweetness of the scrolls
that Ezekiel and John eat recalls the Psalms. Psalm 19, a hymn in
praise of God's law, describes the commands of God as 'sweeter
also than honey, and drippings of the honeycomb' (Psalm 19.10).
Psalm 119, the longest Psalm and also a hymn of praise to the law
of God, also speaks of the sweetness of God's word: 'How sweet
are your words to my taste, sweeter than honey to my mouth!' (Psalm
119.103). The Psalms, and by referring to them also Ezekiel and
Revelation, use the idea of God's word as sweet to the taste to describe
how God's words and instructions are the true pattern for our lives.

If we follow the ways of God they will be sweet, we will find they are the way our lives are supposed to be.

But the sweetness of the Bible in our mouths is not the whole of the story. For John, the prophet of Revelation, there is bitterness to follow. Ezekiel too follows up the sweetness of the scroll with something less easily digestible. He is also sent to a rebellious people in exile, and says: 'I went in bitterness in the heat of my spirit, the hand of the LORD being strong upon me' (Ezekiel 3.14). The prophet Jeremiah, in the midst of his career as the prophet of doom to Jerusalem, also speaks of this mixture:

> Your words were found, and I ate them,
> and your words became to me a joy and the delight of
>   my heart;
> for I am called by your name, O LORD, God of hosts.
> I did not sit in the company of merrymakers, nor did
>   I rejoice;
> under the weight of your hand I sat alone,
> for you had filled me with indignation.
> Why is my pain unceasing, my wound incurable,
> refusing to be healed?
> Truly, you are to me like a deceitful brook, like waters
>   that fail.   (Jeremiah 15.16–18)

Jeremiah, Ezekiel and John all find that the sweetness of God's words to the taste is soon followed by harder stuff. Living by the ways of God is not an easy option. It runs counter to the prevailing wind of culture. For some, like John, it is dangerous to be described as a Christian at all. For others, like Ezekiel, it is hard and difficult work to live out the vision of the Bible. But neither John nor Ezekiel, nor any of the writers of the Bible, will allow us simply to read and go back to life as normal. They all insist this is a book that must be eaten.

Daily bread

Regularly reading the Bible is an important part of how we can eat this book. The Bible provides great feasts but it also provides nourishment for our daily lives. This regular feeding on the Bible is what enables us to be fed. There are lots of ways we can make reading the Bible a regular part of our lives. Perhaps most obviously, if you go regularly to a church, you will hear the Bible read. Often that will be accompanied by a sermon, a reflection or some other kind of exploration of the Bible reading. An important thing to remember is that you don't have to agree with the sermon, even if it is one of mine! It is far more important to work out why you disagree and what you think the Bible readings were about.

Another way of making reading the Bible a regular part of life is to join a group that reads the Bible together and discusses what it is about. Many churches will have groups for Bible reading, but there is nothing to stop you starting a group and inviting friends to join you in reading the Bible together. Reading with other people is a great way to read. It means you will get more than one point of view. It is quite all right to come to a different conclusion from a friend. As you try to explain what you think something means, and listen to what your friend thinks, you will both learn more and understand more about the story you are reading.

Reading the Bible yourself is also part of making the Bible a regular ingredient in life. It can be a daunting idea to reach for the Bible and read some of it. I hope that this book has helped make that less daunting and more exciting. There are plenty of resources available to help you read the Bible regularly. A really helpful one is a set of Bible reading notes. These are produced by a number of different groups but a good place to start would be the Bible Reading Fellowship or Scripture Union (see below under 'Further reading' for details). They each produce notes in many forms: as a printed booklet, online, in audio, by email and as a smartphone app. Some more places to find similar resources are listed at the end of this chapter. Reading with the help of notes helps in deciding which passage to read and provides a guide to read with. They can even help you pray with the passage that you read.

In all these different ways of reading the Bible regularly, remember the ten – actually eleven – 'commandments' for Bible reading that I set out in Chapter 1. They are as follows:

1 pray;
2 find a good translation;
3 read in small bits;
4 read in large chunks;
5 read aloud;
6 get to know the stories;
7 see how the Bible reads itself;
8 read with other people;
9 be prepared to be changed;
10 wrestle;
11 read it!

These commandments are a set of practices that will help you read the Bible and help you get more from reading it. That is all they are – a set of practices. On their own they mean very little – they need to be practised!

Bread and wine

If there is one conversation in the whole of the Bible on which I would like to eavesdrop, it is that between Jesus and two of his disciples as they walk away from Jerusalem to the village of Emmaus on the first Easter day. The whole story can be found in Luke's Gospel (24.13–35). The two disciples' conversation starts in despair. They have given up, thinking that Jesus' death has brought an end to all for which they had hoped. Then a stranger joins them, asks them questions and explains why the Messiah had to suffer and die before rising to a new life. This is a conversation about the Bible. When they reach the house to which they were walking, the disciples invite this stranger to come in and share a meal. Sitting at table, the stranger takes bread, blesses and breaks it. Suddenly the disciples realize that it was Jesus who had joined them. In that moment Jesus vanishes and they return to Jerusalem to rejoin the other disciples.

This is the quintessential story about reading the Bible and it demonstrates many of the practices contained in the ten 'commandments' for Bible reading in action. (The only one missing is commandment 2 – find a good translation.) First, there is prayer (commandment 1) in the story: the prayer of blessing that Jesus prays and in which the disciples' eyes are opened and they recognize who is sitting with them. The story happens on the Sabbath, the day of prayer and rest.

Jesus and the disciples talk about the Bible, from Moses and the prophets through the whole sweep of the story. This is both reading in small bits and reading in large chunks (commandments 3 and 4) as each is explained and slotted into the larger story of the Bible. Knowing the stories within the Bible (commandment 6) is essential to this. This is a conversation conducted out loud (commandment 5). This enables new things to be noticed. It is a conversation conducted between three people, reading with others (commandment 8) in a way that means a completely new understanding is reached.

But above all, this is the Bible reading the Bible (commandment 7) as we see Jesus explaining it to his disciples. There is a great deal of wrestling happening (commandment 10) as the disciples begin by trying to come to terms with the devastating events of Jesus' death, and then have to come to terms with a new way of reading the Bible given to them by the risen Jesus. The result is that they are changed (commandment 9) – they literally change direction and instead of moving away from Jerusalem and the other disciples, they head towards them. Finally, this conversation and others like it provoke many more readings of the Bible (commandment 11). Some of them are collected as the New Testament. Others are still happening.

On the road to Emmaus, the Bible is read. The readers are changed as together they wrestle with the stories of the Bible. It is in prayer that they recognize who has been with them, and then they go to start new ways of life and new ways of reading. This is a story about how to read the Bible.

Food for the journey

The story of the road to Emmaus (Luke 24.13–35), together with the story of Jacob wrestling the angel at Peniel (Genesis 32.22–32), are two of the most important stories that help us understand how to read the Bible. Both are stories of difficulty and hope. In the first, two people have their lives literally turned around as they start to regain hope after despair. In the second, a man struggles until dawn but finally receives a blessing. Both these stories show us the Bible as a book that makes demands on us and involves our own participation. Neither offers us simple instructions or pious sentiment. Rather they ask for our honest engagement with the deepest – and sometimes the darkest – parts of our humanity.

Reading the Bible does not mean to surrender our intelligence and adopt a view of life that thinks the world was made in six days, genocide is justifiable or that God does not want gay people. It is to read a collection of witnesses to the relationship between God and his people, and to be invited to see that we too are witnesses of this ongoing relationship. The Bible is a conversation that we are invited to join. It is a wrestling match in which we are to participate. It is a story within which we are invited to find our story. It is full of argument, difficulty, hope, sex, pain, love, betrayal, prayer, anger, power, corruption, nobility and inspiration. In short, it is full of life. The Bible is a lively and life-giving book. The conversation, the wrestling match and the story continue. We are invited to join them and to find our place within.

It all begins with reading. Make sure your brain is fully engaged.

Try it out

1 Try using some Bible reading notes.
2 Read the Bible!

Further reading

Bible Reading Fellowship: <www.biblereadingnotes.org.uk>.

Scripture Union: <www.scriptureunion.org.uk>.

Another daily reading resource is *Reflections for Daily Prayer* produced by Church House Publishing in print and as a smartphone app: <www.chpublishing.co.uk/features/reflections-for-daily-prayer>.

Notes

Introduction

1 From <www.oremus.org/liturgy/coronation/cor1953b.html>.

1 How to read the Bible

1 Thomas Paine, 'A Letter to the Hon. Thomas Erskine on the Prosecution of Thomas Williams for Publishing the Age of Reason', printed 1797.

2 Dietrich Bonhoeffer, *The Way to Freedom: Letters, Lectures and Notes from the Collected Works*, ed. Edwin H. Robertson, London: Collins, 1966, pp. 237–8.

3 Pat Alexander and Leon Baxter, *The Lion First Bible*, Oxford: Lion Hudson, 1997; Bob Hartman and Krisztina Kallai Nagy, *The Lion Storyteller Bible*, Oxford: Lion Hudson, 2008.

4 Eugene Peterson, *Eat This Book: A Conversation in the Art of Spiritual Reading*, Grand Rapids, MI: Eerdmans, 2006, p. 44.

5 Louis de Bernières, Introduction in *The Book of Job: Authorised King James Version*, Edinburgh: Canongate, 1998, p. xiii.

2 What is the Bible?

1 Diarmaid MacCulloch, *Silence: A Christian History*, London: Penguin, 2013, p. 11.

2 Martin Luther, *Preface to the New Testament*, 1522, in *The Works of Martin Luther*, vol. 6, trans. C. M. Jacobs, Philadelphia, PA: Muhlenberg Press, 1932, p. 444.

3 The story of the Bible

1 Brian D. McLaren, *The Story We Find Ourselves In: Further Adventures of a New Kind of Christian*, London: SPCK, 2013.

2 N. T. Wright, *The New Testament and the People of God*, London: SPCK, 1992, p. 140; emphasis in original.

3 NRSV, alternative wording.

4 Francis Spufford, *Unapologetic: Why, Despite Everything, Christianity Can Still Make Surprising Emotional Sense*, London: Faber & Faber, 2012, p. 29.

4 The stories of Jesus

1 *Watchwords for the Warfare of Life* – see <www.forgottenbooks.com/books/ Watchwords_for_the_Warfare_of_Life_1000572916>.

6 'In the beginning': creation in the Bible

1 Steve Jones, *The Serpent's Promise: The Bible Retold as Science*, London: Little, Brown, 2013, p. 19.

2 Terry Pratchett, *The Last Continent*, London: Doubleday, 1998, p. 10.

3 This is my own paraphrase, based on Alexander Heidel, *The Babylonian Genesis: The Story of Creation*, 2nd edn, Chicago: University of Chicago Press, 1951.

4 Roger Ruston, *Human Rights and the Image of God*, London: SCM Press, 2004, pp. 287–8.

5 This account owes a lot to Bill Bryson, *A Short History of Nearly Everything*, New York: Broadway Books, 2003, with just a dash of Douglas Adams.

7 Difficult subjects 1: money

1 Jim Wallis, *God's Politics: Why the Right Gets It Wrong and the Left Doesn't Get It*, Oxford: Lion, 2006, p. 214.

2 Peter Selby, *An Idol Unmasked: A Faith Perspective on Money*, London: Darton, Longman & Todd, 2014, p. 79.

8 Difficult subjects 2: sex

1 Jo Ind, *Memories of Bliss: God, Sex and Us*, London: SCM Press, 2010, p. 133.

2 In Lawrence H. Schiffman, *Texts and Traditions: A Source Reader for the Study of Second Temple and Rabbinic Judaism*, Hoboken, NJ: KTAV Publishing House, p. 120.

3 Clare Amos, *The Book of Genesis*, Peterborough: Epworth, 2004, p. 22.

9 Difficult subjects 3: violence and the Bible

1 Carolyn Forché, from 'Prayer', in *Blue Hour*, Tarset: Bloodaxe, 2003; <www.bloodaxebooks.com>.

2 Regina M. Schwartz, *The Curse of Cain: The Violent Legacy of Monotheism*, Chicago and London: University of Chicago Press, 1997, p. 31.

3 Schwartz, *Curse of Cain*, p. 176.

4 Phyllis Trible, *Texts of Terror: Literary-Feminist Readings of Biblical Narratives*, London: SCM Press, 1984, p. xiii.

5 Trible, *Texts of Terror*, p. 28.

6 Trible, *Texts of Terror*, p. 87.

7 Trible, *Texts of Terror*, p. 4.

8 Marc H. Ellis, *Unholy Alliance: Religion and Atrocity in Our Time*, London: SCM Press, 1997, p. xvi.

9 René Girard, *Things Hidden Since the Foundation of the World*, trans. Stephen Bann and Michael Metteer, Stanford, CA: Stanford University Press, 1987, p. 104.

10 'Eat this book': the Bible in our lives

1 William Sloane Coffin, 'The Authority of the Bible', in *The Heart Is a Little to the Left: Essays on Public Morality*, Hanover, NH: University Press of New England for Dartmouth College, 1999, p. 49.